SUPER START-THE-SCHOOL-YEAR BOOK

Interactive Games, Bulletin Boards, Poems, Playlets, Art Activities and More!

by

Meish Goldish

SCHOLASTIC

PROFESSIONAL BOOKS

New York • Toronto • London • Auckland • Sydney

Designed by Intergraphics
Cover design by Vincent Ceci
Cover photograph by Richard Hutchings
Illustrations by Joe Chicko, Jane McCreary

ISBN 0-590-49101-6

12 11 10 9 8 7 6 5 4 3 2   2 3 4 5/9

Printed in the U.S.A.

CONTENTS

Introduction 4

1. First-Day Suggestions 5

2. Classroom Rules and Routines 20

3. Name Games and Activities 36

4. Getting to Know Each Other 51

5. Learning About New Places 61

6. Fun for the Whole Class 70

7. Partner and Small-Group Activities 85

8. Individual Student Activities 96

9. Bulletin Board Ideas 107

INTRODUCTION

The start of the school year is critical for students and teachers alike. For the teacher, it is a time to discover students' abilities and interests, to initiate classroom procedures and routines, and to set a tone for learning that will prevail throughout the year. For students, it is a time to meet new classmates, to adjust to an unfamiliar environment, and to find out exactly what is expected of them in the classroom.

To some degree, the success that you and your children enjoy the first few weeks of school will determine your success for the rest of the year. Starting off with fun-filled, imaginative activities is important. That's why *Super Start-The-School-Year Book* is such an asset.

The activities in this book include a wide variety of games, songs, playlets, crafts, bulletin board projects, ways to celebrate birthdays, and other creative ideas—all designed to make the beginning of school a great success. Activities have been grouped so that you can find the perfect one in a snap. The opening section, "First-Day Suggestions," offers a potpourri of creative ideas for that crucial first day of class. Even if you wanted to, you could not cover all the offerings in a single day. Good news: These activities can also be saved for days to come.

Other sections of the book provide innovative ways to introduce classroom rules and routines, help students learn each other's names, discover classmates' backgrounds and interests, and familiarize children with the school building. The final three sections of the book suggest many ways for new students to work together with partners and in small groups, and independently.

We know that *Super Start-The-School-Year Book* will live up to its title, enabling you to enjoy early success that will surely stretch to the very end of the school year.

FIRST-DAY SUGGESTIONS

◆ —————————— ◆

1 DAY

FIRST-DAY CHALLENGE

The first day of school, you will need time to fill out forms and distribute materials to each student. A great way to occupy the class during this time is with a chart, such as the one below.

Make a copy for each child. Explain that the object of the game is to fill in each box with one answer. The answer must fit the category at the top and must start with the letter at the left. For example, students should write the name of a food starting with the letter "F" in the box in the upper left-hand corner. See if students can fill in the entire chart.

As an extension activity, challenge your students to list as many answers for each box as they can. Later, call on volunteers to share their answers with the class.

	Food	TV show or movie	Famous person	Clothing	City, state, province, or country
F					
I					
R					
S					
T					
D					
A					
Y					

GIANT COOPERATIVE JIGSAW PUZZLE

No teacher wants to see a new class go to pieces on the first day—unless, of course, the pieces happen to be part of a jigsaw puzzle! Your students can make this giant puzzle, piece it together, and learn each other's names—all in one fun activity!

To prepare, hang a large sheet of light-colored paper or oaktag, about four feet by four feet, on a classroom door or wall. Have the students take turns writing their names in large letters on the paper. To add variety, each student can use a pen or crayon of a different color.

When everyone is done, remove the signature sheet and cut it into as many pieces as you have children in the class. The pieces should not be perfect squares, but rather triangles, circles, rectangles, or odd shapes. Try to cut them so that a student's entire name does not appear on one piece of the puzzle.

When you are done, distribute one piece of the puzzle to each student. Using an open area on the classroom floor, challenge the class to piece together their names. After it is assembled, tape the puzzle together and display it on a wall.

ANY QUESTIONS?

On the first day of school, students are often bursting with questions about their new environment. Here's a helpful way to handle the situation and have fun in the process:

Hand out five index cards to each student. Tell them to write one question on each card. Questions can be about the school, the classroom, the daily routine, or anything else on their minds. Here are some sample questions:

1. What books will we read this year?
2. How long is recess?
3. Can we bring pets to school?
4. What time is school over?
5. Will we keep the same seats all year?
6. Will we go on a field trip?
7. Where is the lunchroom?
8. Who is the principal?
9. When can we go to the bathroom?
10. What new things will we be learning this year?

Collect all the cards and put them in a box. Pull a card at random and answer the question. Continue the activity as long as it is helpful. For the first week of school, you may wish to spend a few minutes each day answering questions.

Can I bring my snake to school?

MUSICAL INTRODUCTIONS

Here's a musical way for your new students to get to know their classmates' names.

Begin by having each student think of two things she likes, such as pizza and swimming. Each description should be only one word. Then have each student in turn come forward and sing her class introduction to the tune of "Frère Jacques." For example:

> I am Sheri, I am Sheri,
> Yes, I am, Yes, I am.
> I like pizza, I like swimming,
> Yes, I do, Yes, I do.

Then have the class respond by singing:

> You are Sheri, You are Sheri,
> Yes, you are, Yes, you are.
> You like pizza, You like swimming,
> Yes, you do, Yes, you do.

Or try this musical idea: Have your class stand in a circle, and choose one child to be in the middle. Ask students to follow the directions you sing to the tune of "If You're Happy and You Know It":

> If you're Michael, or you know him,
> Clap your hands, [EVERYBODY CLAPS HANDS]
> If you're Michael, or you know him,
> Clap your hands, [EVERYBODY CLAPS HANDS]
> If you're Michael, or you know him,
> And you really want to show him,
> If you're Michael, or you know him,
> Clap your hands. [EVERYBODY CLAPS HANDS]

Then replace the child in the middle with another child. If you like, students in the circle can volunteer to lead each new round of singing.

PARTNER INTRODUCTIONS

At the start of the school year, it's nice to have students introduce themselves. But here's an even nicer procedure: Have students introduce each other! Here's how to do it:

Assign each child a partner. (If you have an odd number of students, form one group of three.) Tell each student to interview his partner by asking the following questions:

1. What is your name?
2. What games do you like to play?
3. What is your favorite movie?
4. What is your favorite school subject?
5. What are your favorite foods?
6. What is your favorite TV show?
7. What are your favorite books?
8. What are your hobbies or favorite activities?
9. What is your favorite color?
10. What is your favorite song?

Students should write down their partner's responses. When the interview is complete, the pair should switch roles. Once all interviews are finished, have your students introduce their partners and share what they have learned.

THIS INTRODUCTION IS A JOKE!

Every class has its comedians. But what do you do when the whole class is full of them? In this enjoyable activity, that's a dilemma you and your children can laugh about. Have each student introduce himself to the class by stating his name and then telling a joke or a riddle. Naturally, give your students time to guess the answers before they are revealed!

As an alternative, have each student relate something humorous that happened to him over the summer.

CLASS PASSPORTS

During the first week of school, your classroom might seem like a foreign country to your students. So why not equip them with passports?

Begin by asking your students if they know what a passport is. Explain that it's a small booklet with a person's photograph and important information about the person, such as where she is from. People need to show their passports when they travel from one country to another. If possible, display a real passport.

Have students make their own passports to use when they enter and leave the classroom. Provide students with photographs of themselves to paste on the first page of their passports. (If no camera is available, have students draw self-portraits.) Ask students to write their names under their pictures.

On other pages of the booklet, have students fill in the following information:

My address is ―――――――――――――――――――――――― .

My telephone number is ―――――――――――――――――― .

My birthday is ―――――――――――――――――――――――― .

My age is ――――――――――――――――――――――――――― .

My room number is ――――――――――――――――――――― .

My teacher is ――――――――――――――――――――――――― .

When students leave or enter your room during the first week of school, request to see their passports. Ask them one piece of information each time, such as "What is your telephone number?" By week's end, kids should be able to identify themselves very well!

CLASSROOM SCAVENGER HUNT

A scavenger hunt is a great way for students to discover interesting facts about their classmates. Distribute a sheet with the questions below to each child. Tell your students they have 15 minutes (more or less if you desire) to answer the questions by circulating among classmates and briefly interviewing each other. Only one name is needed for each blank.

As a variation, have students work in pairs or small groups.

1. Who has a birthday in September? _____

2. Who has more brothers than sisters? _____

3. Who has green eyes? _____

4. Who has red hair? _____

5. Who walks to school every day? _____

6. Who lives within two blocks of school? _____

7. Who has no middle name? _____

8. Who saw the same movie as you this summer? _____

9. Who is new in the school this year? _____

10. Who went to camp this summer? _____

11. Who knows how to bake a cake? _____

12. Who has ridden a horse? _____

13. Who can speak a foreign language? _____

14. Whose favorite color is green? _____

15. Whose favorite ice cream is strawberry? _____

16. Who has a magazine subscription? _____

17. Whose first name starts with M? _____

18. Whose family has a blue car? _____

19. Who is left-handed? _____

20. Who can play the piano? _____

I LOVE ADD-ON GAME

There's a cute poem that goes like this:

> Do you love me
> Or do you not?
> You told me once
> But I forgot.

Can your students remember the things their classmates love? Find out with this simple activity.

Ask one student to introduce himself and then name something he loves. For example:

"My name is Barry and I love little league."

Ask the student next to him to repeat the statement and add a statement of his own.

"His name is Barry and he loves little league. My name is Jason and I love going to the beach."

Then ask a third student to repeat the first two statements and add a statement of her own, and so on. See if anyone in the class can successfully name every classmate and his or her "love."

LETTER COLLAGE

Ask your students if they know what a collage is. Explain that a collage is made by pasting a number of pictures together to make a design. A collage is a good way to show other people what you are interested in.

Have your class make Letter Collages that spell their names. First, distribute a large piece of butcher paper to each child. Tell the students to write the letters of their first name, making each letter big and "thick" (as shown below).

Next, ask students to find magazine pictures of people, places, and things they like. Pictures can include favorite foods, sports, clothing, hobbies, TV celebrities, or vacation spots. Each picture must be small enough to fit inside the letters they have outlined. Have students paste the pictures they've selected inside the letters of their names. When complete, they've got a giant name collage!

Display the name collages on the classroom walls. Let each student stand next to her name and tell why she chose each picture.

ABC LINE UP

What's a good way to have your students meet their classmates while they practice their ABCs? Try this challenging activity:

Randomly select a student, calling her by her last name ("Ms. Jones, please"). Ask that student to come forward and face the classroom door. Then call a second student by his last name. Tell the students to line up in alphabetical order by their *first* names. Students may need to ask classmates their first names, if they don't already know them. (No help from the teacher!) Then call a third student, a fourth student, and so on.

The object is to end up with the entire class lined up alphabetically by first name. Then see if anyone can remember the first name of everyone in line!

TAKING THE CLASS CENSUS

Ask your students if they know what a census is. Explain that it is a count of all the people who live in one country. In the United States, a census is taken every ten years. Citizens are asked to fill out a form with many questions on it. Their answers are tallied up to help the government set up programs that will benefit them.

Distribute a "census form" to your students. Tell them that the information they fill out will help you plan for a great school year. The form might look something like this:

Name _____

Date of birth _____

How many people are in your family? _____

What are their names? _____

What pets do you have at home? _____

What subject do you like best in school? (check one)

          _____ reading   _____ arithmetic

          _____ spelling   _____ social studies

What are your hobbies or favorite activities? _____

What sports do you like most? _____

What is your favorite food? _____

What is your favorite book? _____

What TV shows do you like to watch? _____

Who are your best friends? _____

If you had $100, what would you do with it? _____

_____

Each day, select one questionnaire and read it to the class. See if they can guess which classmate filled it out. As with a real census, tally up their responses and address the findings. For example, if a large number of students like a certain food perhaps you could serve it at the next birthday party.

BACK-TO-SCHOOL ANIMAL TALK

How would it feel to face a classroom full of animals at the start of school? Find out with this "wild" activity! Have each student find a picture of an animal in a magazine, cut it out, and paste it on a sheet of white paper. If magazines aren't available your kids can draw the animals.

Then ask, "What might this animal say on its first day of school?" Offer a few examples, such as:

A dog might say: "The first day of school was ru-u-u-f-f-f!"
A cat might say: "The first day of school was purr-fect!"
A lion might say: "The first day was great. I'm not lion!"
A fish might say: "I love a school!"

Tell each student to draw a speech balloon coming out of the animal's mouth and to write in it what the animal is saying. Later, have the class share their pictures and sayings aloud, or display them on a bulletin board.

PUT YOUR FEET ON THE DESK!

What teacher in her right mind would encourage students to put their feet on the desk? Yet that's exactly what you do in this activity! Start by having students remove their shoes and socks. Ask them to step onto colored construction paper and trace around each foot. Then tell them to cut out the "feet," writing their first name on the left foot and their last name on the right foot. Finally, have students tape the feet to the back of their desk. That way, they can keep their feet on the desk all year long!

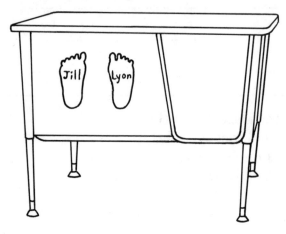
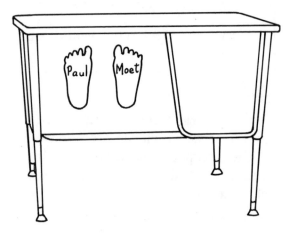

Here's a work of art your students can create together that will bring cheer to your classroom all year long.

To start, take a large black-and-white or color photo from a magazine. Cut the picture into as many squares as you have children in your class. Number the back of the squares so you will know how to piece them together to recreate the original picture.

Distribute one square to each student. Then have the student take an eight-inch (20 centimeters by 20 centimeters) square of plain white paper and, with crayons or colored pencils, reproduce the portion of the picture that he received. When everyone is finished, collect all the drawings. On the classroom wall, piece them together according to number. You will be surprised how much this blown-up class picture resembles the original magazine photo!

THE CHILDREN ON THE BUS

Many of your students will ride the bus home every day. For the first week or so, younger children in particular may be unsure about which bus to board. Issuing bus passes or tags is one way to handle the problem. Posting a bus chart on your wall is another. But have you considered a musical solution?

Tell the class to form a circle and ask one of the "bus children" to stand in the middle. Sing her this song to the tune of "The Wheels on the Bus":

> Oh, Jenny's on the bus that's number 9,
> Number 9, number 9,
> Yes, Jenny's on the bus that's number 9,
> Riding from school.

If singing a separate verse for each child takes too long, combine two names into one verse, such as:

> Oh, Dan's on the bus that's number 4,
> Number 4, number 4,
> And Sharon's on the bus that's number 4,
> Riding from school.

By the end of the week, your students will not only know their own bus numbers, but probably those of their classmates' as well. If some members of your class walk home from school, you can create a verse especially for them, such as:

> Oh, Kathy walks right to her door,
> To her door, to her door,
> Yes Kathy walks right to her door,
> Walking home from school.

FIRST-DAY OPINION POLL

The first day of class, some students may feel like they're all thumbs. Fortunately, thumbs can come in "handy" in helping you understand your students' thoughts and feelings about the first day of school.

At the end of the first day, give a copy of the form below to each student. Tell the children to draw a *thumbs up* next to the things they like and a *thumbs down* next to the things they don't like.

Once you have read the completed forms, spend some time with your students, either as a group or individually, discussing their comments.

THUMBS UP, THUMBS DOWN

Name _____

If something was good, draw

If something was bad, draw

My desk	Reading
My books	Arithmetic
My supplies	Lunch
The classroom pets	Recess
The classroom decorations	The bus

CLASSROOM RULES
AND ROUTINES

WHO NEEDS RULES? PLAYLET

Perform this playlet early in the school year to help show your new students the importance of following rules.

Assign each student a part. The Chorus can be made up of as many students as you wish. Parts are as follows:

Narrator	Chorus
Rule Reciters:	Rule Breakers:
Rule #1	Latecomer
Rule #2	Mr. or Ms. Messy
Rule #3	Jabbermouth
Rule #4	Hall-Runner
Rule #5	Line-Pusher
Rule #6	RoughHouser
Rule #7	Bus Show-Off

Ask the Narrator, Rule Reciters, and Rule Breakers to read their lines in turn. (Each Rule Reciter should also hold up a sign with the pertinent classroom rule written on it, for example, "Be on time.") Then have the Chorus sing each classroom lesson to the tune of "Twinkle, Twinkle, Little Star."

NARRATOR: Welcome to our classroom play.
It tells of rules we must obey.
You have to follow every rule.
If you don't, you'll be a fool!
Let us see what comes to pass
When rules are broken in our class.

RULE #1: Rule number one: Be on time. (Holds up a sign that says "Be on Time.")

LATECOMER: I am Latecomer, late to school.
I thought being late was cool.
But then I missed the work assigned,
And now I've fallen way behind!

NARRATOR: Latecomer broke an important rule. What can we learn from his mistake?

CHORUS: Be on time to school each day,
You'll know what to do that way.
Class can be a lot of fun
If you're here when the day's begun.
Be on time and don't be late,
Watch the clock and you'll feel great!

WHO NEEDS RULES? PLAYLET (continued)

NARRATOR:	Now let's see what comes to pass When *another* rule is broken in class.
RULE #2:	Rule number two: Be neat when you work. (Holds up a sign that says "Be Neat.")
MR. MESSY:	I'm Mr. Messy all day long. I never care what I do wrong. But once with paint I made a mess And spilled it on my classmate's dress!
NARRATOR:	Uh, oh! Mr. Messy broke another important rule. What can we learn from his mistake?
CHORUS:	When you're working, do be neat, Don't be messy at your seat. Careful, careful what you take, No one wants a spill or break. Don't be messy, just be neat When you're working at your seat.
NARRATOR:	Here's a third rule you should know, If you break it, oh, oh, oh!
RULE #3:	Rule number three: Listen closely when someone is speaking. (Holds up a sign that says "Listen Closely.")
JABBERMOUTH:	I'm Jabbermouth, I talk all day, I never hear what people say. But once, on a walk, I got a fright, The class turned left, and I turned right!
NARRATOR:	Jabbermouth was lost because she didn't listen to the teacher's directions. What can we learn from this?
CHORUS:	Listen closely, listen hard, Always keep your ears on guard. Do not speak when others do, They will think it's rude of you. Listen closely, lend an ear, Never miss what you must hear.
NARRATOR:	In the hallway, there's a rule You should never break at school.
RULE #4:	Rule number four: Don't run in the halls. (Holds up a sign that says "Don't Run in the Halls.")

HALL-RUNNER: I'm Hall-Runner, on the run,
Running in the halls is fun.
But one day I ran and tripped,
You should see the pants I ripped!

NARRATOR: Hall-Runner learned his lesson the hard way. What rule did he forget?

CHORUS: In the hallway, do not run,
Falling down is never fun.
Walking is the way to go,
Not too fast, just nice and slow.
Don't go running in the hall,
Make the building safe for all.

NARRATOR: In the lunchroom line each day,
Here's a rule we must obey.

RULE #5: Rule number five: No pushing in the lunchroom line. (Holds up a sign that says "Don't push at lunch.")

LINE-PUSHER: I'm Line-Pusher, at lunch I love
To cut in line and push and shove.
But one day when I tried to push,
I dropped my lunch, and now it's mush!

NARRATOR: Line-Pusher went hungry that day because he broke a school rule. What can we learn from his mistake?

CHORUS: In the lunchroom, do not push,
Or your lunch may turn to mush.
Just be patient, wait in line,
Take your turn and you'll be fine.
Never push, or food may toss,
Apples could be applesauce!

NARRATOR: On the playground, there's a rule. If you break it, you're a fool.

RULE #6: Rule number six: Don't play rough on the playground. (Holds up sign saying "Don't play rough.")

ROUGHHOUSER: I'm a RoughHouser when I play,
I don't care what others say.
But once I threw Mike in the dirt
And accidentally he got hurt.

NARRATOR: RoughHouser didn't mean to hurt anyone, but he did by breaking an important rule. What should he remember?

CHORUS: On the playground, don't be rough,
Just play nicely, never tough.
Have fun when you're in the yard,
Play your best but not too hard.
Cut the roughhouse when you play,
No one will get hurt that way.

NARRATOR: Our final rule is for all of us
Who come to school on the bus.

RULE #7: Rule number seven: Stay in your seat on the bus. (Holds up a sign that says "Don't Stand on the Bus.")

BUS SHOW-OFF: I'm a Show-Off on the bus,
I walk around and make a fuss.
But one time, when we made a stop,
I fell down and went "KERPLOP!"

NARRATOR: After that accident, Bus Show-Off was very sore. What safety rule did she forget?

CHORUS: On the bus, you must sit down
As the driver drives through town.
Never stand up in the aisle.
You may fall and lose your smile.
On the bus, just keep your seat,
You'll be safe, which can't be beat!

NARRATOR: Those are the rules we must obey
In class, at lunch, or when we play.
You must follow every rule,
If you don't, you'll be a fool.
Now let's have a quick review
So we'll remember what to do.

RULE #1: Be on time.
RULE #2: Be neat.
RULE #3: Listen closely.
RULE #4: Don't run in the halls.
RULE #5: Don't push at lunch.
RULE #6: Don't play rough.
RULE #7: Don't stand on the bus.

ALL STUDENTS: We remember all the rules,
We will keep them—we're no fools!

CLASS-CREATED RULE LIST

Ask your students to imagine there are no stop signs or traffic lights anywhere on the streets. Why might that be dangerous? Help them to understand that street signs and stoplights keep the streets safer, so that fewer accidents occur.

Then ask: "Why do we need rules in our classroom?" (Some students may not know the answer. Help them to understand that classroom rules, like street signs, make things safer by telling children what to do.

Present each of the following hypothetical situations. For each one, ask, "What rule could we invent that would make things better?" (Remember never to use the name of a child in your classroom.) On a large sheet of oaktag, write the rules that the students suggest.

1. Tony threw a baseball in the classroom, and it broke a window.

2. While Ingrid was giving a report, two children were whispering to each other. Ingrid's feelings were hurt.

3. Kevin and Shelli were racing in the hallway. They both tripped and skinned their knees.

4. Carolyn and Kim were coloring. Kim needed the crayon that Carolyn was using, so she grabbed it from Carolyn. Then Carolyn hit Kim.

5. Paul was talking to a friend while the teacher was explaining the homework. Paul didn't hear the assignment.

6. Sue spilled some glue on the worktable and just left it there. Later, Calvin put his paper on the table and the paper got all gooey.

7. Jim spilled juice on his shirt during lunch. Brian saw the stain and told his friends about it. They laughed and made Jim cry.

Challenge your students to come up with more situations where rules are needed. Hang the list of rules in your classroom. Chances are it will be strictly adhered to because the students made the rules themselves.

ATTENDANCE SURVEYS

Most teachers have students answer a roll call with a standard "Here." To spice up this procedure—and learn a little about your students in the process—ask the children to respond to one of the following questions when they hear their names:

On the first day of class: What is your favorite food?
On the second day: What is your favorite TV show or movie?
On the third day: What is your favorite holiday?
On the fourth day: What is your favorite animal?
On the fifth day: What is your favorite game?

The second week of school, you might have students answer these questions at roll call:

On the sixth day: In what city or town were you born?
On the seventh day: What is your favorite school subject?
On the eighth day: When is your birthday?
On the ninth day: Who is your favorite celebrity?
On the tenth day: What color are your eyes?

No doubt you can think of many other lively questions to ask students.

SINGING THE RULES

A fun and effective way to reinforce classroom rules is to have your students sing them! Call on different students to perform (or pantomime) the "action" of each verse, sung to the tune of "Here We Go Round the Mulberry Bush." For example:

> This is the way we sit up straight,
> Sit up straight,
> Sit up straight,
> This is the way we sit up straight,
> When we're in the classroom.

Other verses include:

> This is the way we smile at friends . . .
> This is the way we act polite . . .
> This is the way we pick up trash . . .
> This is the way we walk, don't run . . .
> This is the way we listen well . . .
> This is the way we straighten chairs . . .
> This is the way we hang up coats . . .
> This is the way we open books . . .
> This is the way we talk, not yell . . .

Make up your own verses to suit your individual classroom needs!

RIGHT HERE OR LEFT OUT?

Have you ever wished for a faster way to take attendance? Ever wished for an effective way to teach your students left from right? Here's a great way to do both:

Draw a line down the middle of a large sheet of oaktag board. Label the left side "Left Out" and the right side "Right Here." Make a name tag for each student in your class, or have the students make their own. Laminate the tags and punch a hole through the top of each one.

Next, attach rows of paper clips to the oaktag to create hooks. (Do this by bringing half the paperclip through the board.) You'll need a hook for each child's name on both the Left Out side and the Right Here side.

Have the children move the tags to the Left Out side when they leave the classroom at the end of the day. Have them move the tags to the Right Here side when they enter the classroom each morning.

The benefits? You learn who's in and out, while your students learn left and right.

LEFT OUT | RIGHT HERE

Rob

Terri

Paul

Ann Ken MIKE Ang

Toni Carol Joe Tera Ross

Kelly John Tony Nancy

Jane Rick Maria Jack

WACKY CLASS LINE-UPS

When you're pressed for time, the quickest way to line your students up for classroom exit is probably row by row or desk group by desk group. But if you've got a few extra minutes, why not try one of these fun and unusual methods?

1. Say: "Students who have green anywhere on their socks, please line up . . . now students with red on their socks . . . now students with yellow on their socks . . ." and so on.

2. Say: "Students with only two letters in their first name, please line up . . . now students with three letters . . . four letters . . . five letters . . ." and so on.

3. Say: "Students whose favorite ice cream flavor is rocky road . . . now pistachio . . . peppermint . . . banana . . . strawberry . . . vanilla . . . chocolate . . ." and so on.

4. Say: "Students whose favorite sport is tennis . . . soccer . . . volleyball . . . swimming . . . skiing . . . basketball . . . football . . . baseball . . ." and so on.

5. Say: "Students whose favorite dwarf is Sleepy . . . Dopey . . . Grumpy . . . Sneezy . . . Happy . . . Bashful . . . Doc."

There's no end to the number of categories you can devise for line-up!

CLASSROOM DOOR TRIVIA

Every morning before your students enter the classroom, post a different trivia question on the front door. Challenge your students to find out the answer by the next morning.

Here are some possible questions:

1. Where was Abraham Lincoln born?
2. How old is Mickey Mouse?
3. What is the world's tallest mountain?
4. In what year did this school open?
5. Who was the tenth President of the United States?
6. What famous person was born today?
7. Which state is the smallest?
8. How many inches are in a yard?
9. How old is the automobile?
10. How tall was the tallest man in the world?

Each day, call on a volunteer to give the answer to yesterday's question. Ask them to explain how they found the answer. (If there are no volunteers, be prepared to answer the question yourself!)

BOOK JACKET QUILT

A Book Jacket Quilt is the perfect way to warm students up to reading. Here's how to make one:

Each time a child finishes reading a book, ask her to contribute a square to the quilt. Give her a sheet of construction paper and tell her to write down the book's title and author. Then have her draw her favorite scene from the story on it.

Every time a new "patch" is completed, attach it with tape to the old patches. The quilt will grow as your students read more and more books. Display the quilt on a classroom wall. Encourage your students to peruse it every so often to discover books their classmates have read that they may wish to read too.

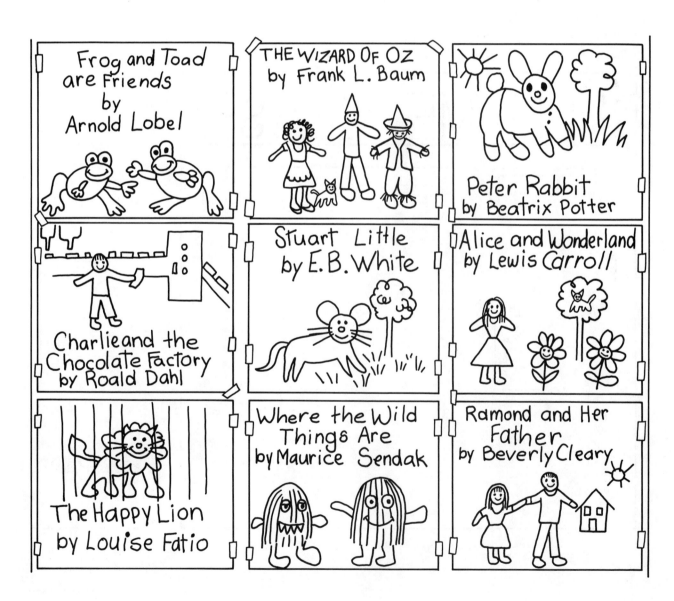

HELP-ME-PLEASE BOARD

On an airplane, passengers who need assistance can press an overhead button to signal the attendant. In a classroom, students who need assistance can post their name on a Help-Me-Please Board to signal you.

Take a wooden board and attach a hook for every student in your class. Label the board "Help Me Please." Then make a name card for each student, keeping all the cards in a box next to the board.

If a student needs help while you are occupied, he simply goes to the Help-Me-Please Board and places his name tag on a hook. When you have a chance, glance at the board to see who needs your assistance.

32

A LOST-AND-FOUND BOX

Your students may start to lose things from the first day of school—things such as gloves, hats, and favorite pens. Cope with the situation by providing a Lost-and-Found Box.

Take a large cardboard box—a television box will do fine—and have students decorate it with colorful construction or contact paper. Label the box "Lost and Found." Instruct your students to put all stray items they find in the box, and you do the same. Then, at the end of each day or every few days, display the items and see how many get claimed!

SUPER ASSIGNMENT BOARD

When students are absent from school it can create problems. Absentees may not know what classwork was missed until they return. That's why it's a good idea to establish an Assignment Board at the beginning of the school year.

Each week, appoint a different student as Assignment Monitor. Have this child list the day's classwork, handouts, and homework on the Assignment Board. The Assignment Monitor should also write down the dates when important papers are due or tests are held.

Of course, it's possible that the Assignment Monitor may be absent on her assigned day, so be sure to designate a substitute.

YEAR-LONG JOURNALS

Why not ask each of your students to write a book? Writing a whole book may sound like a difficult task for young children, but it's really not hard if they get a chance to work on it a little bit each week.

Starting the first week of school, have your students devote a few minutes each day or every few days to writing in journals. Explain that all journal writing will be strictly confidential and read only by the teacher. The first entry might be about their initial impressions of the school and their classes. Later journal entries can be about anything on their minds such as:

- personal experiences
- funny incidents
- scary moments
- exciting times
- hopes and wishes
- unusual dreams
- personal thoughts
- things learned in school

By the end of the school year, students may be surprised to discover they have each written a whole book!

PERSONAL DICTIONARIES

Ask your students if they've ever heard of Noah Webster. Explain that, in 1828, Noah Webster published the first dictionary in the United States. How many words were listed in the first dictionary? There were about 70,000, which may sound like a lot. But the dictionary today has over 450,000 words!

Ask your students: "Why do you think there are more words in a dictionary today than there were in 1828?" Explain that early dictionaries listed only rare or difficult words. Then tell your students they can make their own dictionaries of difficult words.

Begin this activity by asking students to staple or clip together 26 sheets of ruled paper. Have them write one letter of the alphabet at the top of each page. Then during the school year, whenever students come across a new word—in reading or in conversation—they enter it on the correct page of their dictionaries. Older students may write the meaning next to the word, or write a sample sentence.

By the end of the year, each student will have compiled a personal dictionary of new words!

SUPERHERO OF THE WEEK

Children love superheros. So why not give each of your students the opportunity to be the Superhero of the Week?

Each Friday afternoon, announce who will be next week's Superhero. Tell that student to come in Monday with a bag full of items that tell about himself. The bag's contents might include family photos; favorite small toys; stamps, coins, stickers, or other hobby items; pictures of favorite movie or TV stars; postcards from places traveled; or photos of pets.

On Monday, have the Superhero show the bag contents to classmates and talk about each item. Encourage the listeners to ask questions at the end of the presentation.

You can also prepare a special bulletin board honoring the Superhero of the Week. Let one group of students design a colorful name plate for the honoree. The letters might be formed from glitter and glue, or outlined in colorful yarn. Let another group of students compose a poem about the Superhero, telling why he's so special. The remainder of your students can draw pictures of the Superhero involved in his favorite activities.

Put all of the creations on the bulletin board, along with a sheet of paper headed "Why I Like Our Superhero." Encourage children to contribute comments to the paper throughout the week.

A few privileges you can award the Superhero are: On Monday, let the Superhero sit at your desk for a while. On Tuesday, invite the Superhero to have lunch with you. On Wednesday, have the Superhero lead the line leaving class. On Thursday, give the Superhero a few extra minutes of play time. On Friday, have the Superhero wear a special crown or cape.

FUNNY-ANECDOTE TAPES

Children love to tell others of their humorous experiences. Here's a way for your students to share them with the whole class.

During the school year, assign a different student each week to be the class "Humor Recorder." At a designated time, have that child go around the room and record the funny anecdotes of her classmates. Set aside a half hour or so of Laugh Time at the end of the week. Then play back the tape for the class to enjoy.

NAME GAMES AND ACTIVITIES

MY NAME IS
_____

MUSICAL NAME CHAIN

   Your students are sure to enjoy this musical activity designed to help them get acquainted with their classmates names.

   Ask your class to sit in a circle. Choose one student (Melissa, for example) to stand outside it. Then have that child walk around the circle while everyone sings the following song to the tune of "The Farmer in the Dell":

> Melissa's in the class,
> Melissa's in the class,
> Hi-ho, the dairy-o,
> Melissa's in the class.

Melissa then chooses someone to hold her hand and walk around the circle with her. The class sings:

> Melissa chooses Kevin,
> Melissa chooses Kevin,
> Hi-ho, the dairy-o,
> Melissa chooses Kevin.

Kevin then chooses someone to join him and Melissa.

> Kevin chooses Mark,
> Kevin chooses Mark . . .

Continue the song and activity until all students in the class are holding hands and walking in a circle together.

WHAT'S IN A NAME GAME

Ask your students this riddle: "What belongs to you, but other people use it more than you do?" The answer: Your name! This activity lets your students use their classmates' names in a creative exercise.

Ask each student to write his first and last name at the top of a piece of paper. Collect the papers and redistribute them at random. (If anyone gets his own paper back, have him switch with someone else.)

Challenge the students to create as many words as they can from the letters in the name at the top of the page. You can set a time limit such as five minutes, or allow children to take it home overnight.

When the activity is complete, have each student read the name he received and the words he made from the letters of that name.

Jana	Palmer
lap	are
pal	mare
pan	real
men	am
ran	paler
male	rap
jam	near

THE NAME RHYMING GAME

This delightful activity teaches your students about rhyming words while familiarizing them with their classmates!

With the class in a circle, have one student begin by saying to the classmate next to her, "My name is _____ and it rhymes with _____ ." For example:

"My name is Beth and it rhymes with breath."

or

If the student can't think of a real word to rhyme with his name, a nonsense rhyme will also do. For example:

"My name is David and it rhymes with shavid."

The second student repeats the first student's rhyme and adds one of his own. For example:

"Her name is Beth and it rhymes with breath. My name is Mark and it rhymes with shark."

Then the third student repeats the second student's rhyme and adds one of her own. Continue around the circle until everyone has participated. Challenge older children to try to repeat *all* the previous names and rhymes before adding their own. Can anyone in class remember *everyone's* name and rhyming word?

CLASS LIST SPELLING BEE

Your students will love this special spelling bee designed to help them remember their classmates' names. The procedure is simple:

Have everyone stand up. Then select a student and give her the first name of a classmate to spell. If she spells it correctly, give her another name to spell, and so on. If a student misspells a name, ask her to sit down, and choose another student to spell it.

If you run out of first names, use students' last names or middle names. The winner of the spelling bee is the last student left standing in the room.

WORD SEARCH PUZZLE

Your students will love hunting for their names in this custom-made word search puzzle.

On a piece of plain paper (or graph paper) create a puzzle, such as the one below, that contains each of your students' first names. The names can run horizontally, vertically, and/or diagonally. Make copies and distribute one to each child. Then see who's first to circle all the names. If it's very early in the year, you might want to provide students with a list of class members.

A	L	J	O	H	N	P	E	P	A	M	E	L	A
R	I	O	T	E	A	K	A	R	E	N	A	N	N
T	E	D	H	A	N	K	O	R	S	O	N	U	D
I	W	I	L	L	I	A	M	A	T	J	E	R	I
E	V	E	N	Y	C	L	O	V	I	S	T	S	E
L	U	M	E	I	S	H	S	A	R	A	H	G	E
B	R	I	A	N	B	A	R	B	A	R	A	K	L

LINKING-NAME GAME

Here's a unique activity that challenges students to link the letters of their names to those of their classmates.

Write the first names of all your students on the chalkboard or on a sheet of paper that you duplicate for everyone in your class. Give each child a piece of graph paper, making sure its "boxes" are big enough for your students to write letters inside. (If such graph paper is not available you can make your own.)

Challenge your students to cross as many names as possible. The names can be crossed either horizontally or vertically. See if anyone can link three, four, or more names together. Can anyone link the entire class?

							S	A	R	A	H	
		M	I	K	E					L		
			Y				J	U	D	Y		
			L				O			C		
B	R	U	C	E		S	T	E	P	H	E	N

PERSONALIZED TONGUE TWISTERS

Ask your student's if they know what a tongue twister is. See how easily they can recite any of these classics:

"She sells seashells by the seashore."

"Rubber baby buggy bumpers."

"Peter Piper picked a peck of pickled peppers. A peck of pickled peppers did Peter Piper pick."

Then ask your students to invent their own tongue twisters using the sound of the beginning of their first names. Challenge the class to write sentences in which every word (or almost every word) starts with that sound. Sentences may be serious or silly. For example:

Billy blows big blue bubbles.

Terry tickles ten tiny toes.

Joey jumps on joyful jelly beans.

Carrie cooks crumbly cranberry cakes quickly.

When students are finished, have volunteers write their tongue twisters on the chalkboard. Challenge students to recite each tongue twister five times rapidly without tripping over the words!

Find out who the Tongue Twister Champion is in your class!

SING THAT NAME!

Your class might be interested to know that the famous composer Mozart was writing music at the age of five! While your students may not be prepared to write symphonies, they *are* ready to create song lyrics about their names.

Select a student. Then have the class sing about his name to the tune of "Bingo." For example:

> There's someone special in our class,
> And Bobby is his name, oh,
> B-O-B-B-Y,
> B-O-B-B-Y,
> B-O-B-B-Y,
> And Bobby is his name, oh!

Continue singing verses until everyone's name has been spelled out in song.

As a special challenge, have the class clap hands instead of singing the first letter. For example:

> There's someone special in our class,
> And Jane is her name, oh,
> [CLAP] A-N-E,
> [CLAP] A-N-E,
> [CLAP] A-N-E,
> And Jane is her name, oh!

NAME BINGO

Looking for a great way to teach students their classmates' names? How about a game of bingo! Here's how it works:

Prepare a full-page version of the Bingo card shown below. If your class has fewer than 25 children, create a 16-square card (4 rows of 4) or a 9-square card (3 rows of 3). Duplicate one copy for each child. Gather a sufficient number of beans or buttons to use as markers.

Write all of the first names of your class members on slips of paper and put them in a bag. Also list the names on the board for your students to see. (If two students have the same name be sure to add the first letter of their last name.) Tell the children to write each of the names in a different box on their bingo cards—they choose the configurations.

When each child has filled in all 25 boxes, you are ready to play. Pull a name from the bag and read it aloud. Students who have that name on their cards should cover it with a marker. Continue pulling names and reading them aloud until someone has covered five squares in a row. That child should call "Classroom Bingo!" and then read the five names aloud for you to verify. Children whose names are called should stand up and identify themselves.

You may wish to play a second- or third-place winner before clearing the cards and starting a new round. Be sure to save the cards for future games.

Classroom Bingo

Luke	Angela	Rob	Mike	Kelli
Ross	Tera	Nancy	Joe	Anna
José	Rochelle	Megan	Jessie	Lauren
Roberta	Rick	Terri	Carol	Jeremy
Heather	John	Tony	Paul	Becky

44

THE PRICE OF NAMES GAME

This double-fun activity helps students sharpen their math skills while they learn their classmates' names.

Put your students' names on the board along with the following chart:

A	B	C	D	E	F	G	H	I	J	K	L	M
1¢	2¢	3¢	4¢	5¢	6¢	7¢	8¢	9¢	10¢	11¢	12¢	13¢

N	O	P	Q	R	S	T	U	V	W	X	Y	Z
14¢	15¢	16¢	17¢	18¢	19¢	20¢	21¢	22¢	23¢	24¢	25¢	26¢

Instruct each child to use the chart to figure out the price of his name. For example, the name PAUL would cost 16¢ + 1¢ + 21¢ + 12¢ = 50¢. Have each student write the amount next to his name on the board.

Then pass out a sheet with these questions on it for students to answer:

1. Whose name costs the most?
2. Whose name costs the least?
3. Whose names cost less than 50¢?
4. Whose names cost more than 60¢?
5. Can you think of the name that would cost exactly 75¢?
6. What is the most expensive name you can think of?
7. What is the least expensive name you can think of?

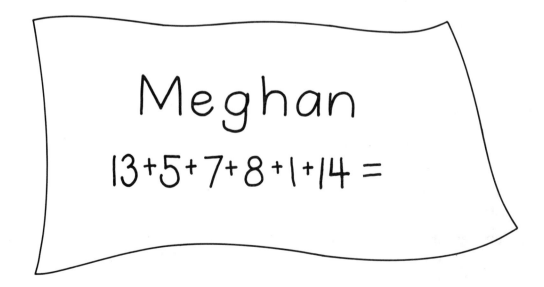

CODED NAMES

This variation on The Price of Names Game will turn your children into secret agents! Prepare a chart similar to the one previously used, but do not place a ¢ sign at the end of each number.

On the board, write a student's name in code. For example, BARRY would be 2-1-18-18-25.

First ask if anyone can figure out whose name is in code without referring to the chart. If no one can, have the class decode the first letter. Continue to decode the letters until someone can identify the name.

Repeat the procedure using several students' names. Pretty soon, your children will know everyone's name—and have their numbers too!

SELF-NAMED INVENTIONS

Write these words on the chalkboard:

- a sandwich
- a saxophone
- a leotard
- a cardigan sweater
- a diesel engine
- braille

Ask your students if they know what the words have in common. Tell them that each item listed was named after its inventor.

The *sandwich* was named after the Earl of Sandwich.
The *saxophone* was invented by Adolphe Sax.
The *leotard* was designed by Jules Leotard.
The *cardigan* was first worn by the Earl of Cardigan.
The *diesel* engine was invented by Rudolph Diesel.
Braille was developed by Louis Braille.

If other people can name inventions after themselves, so can your students. Challenge your children to draw pictures of original inventions and to name them after themselves.
Offer these name-inventions as examples:

- Mike-rowave
- Dustinbuster
- Marilynmatic
- Wallypaper
- Cindyspoon
- Ritawriter

When your students are finished, invite them to share their name-inventions with the entire class. Afterwards, hang all pictures in a Gallery of Class Inventions.

NAME SOMETHING GAME

This challenging name game will stimulate your students' creativity. Begin by asking the class, "Can you name something green?" Go around the room and have the students give their names followed by an answer. For example:

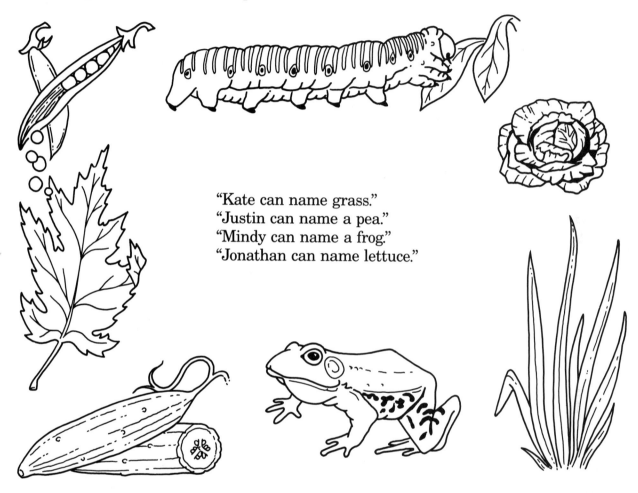

"Kate can name grass."
"Justin can name a pea."
"Mindy can name a frog."
"Jonathan can name lettuce."

If a child is momentarily stumped, tell her to raise her hand when she thinks of something, and go on to the next student. See if everyone in the class can come up with a different answer.

Other categories include:

"Can you name something to wear?"
. . . . something made of wood?"
. . . . something with corners?"
. . . . something bigger than you?"
. . . . something you eat with a spoon?"

Students will also enjoy making up their own categories.

NAME CONCENTRATION

Here's a fun game that will help your students match their classmates' names to their classmates' faces.

To prepare, take a Polaroid picture of each student in your class. Cut pieces of paper so that they are the same size as the photos—one for every student in class. Write each student's name on a piece of that paper. Shuffle the photos and names, and number their backs. Then tack them facedown in rows on the bulletin board.

Now you're ready to play. Divide the class into two teams. Ask the first player on Team A to call out two numbers. Turn over those two squares. If the photo and name match, award the team one point. If the photo and name don't match, turn them over and give a player on Team B a turn.

Since students will probably remember the location of their own pictures and names after they have seen them, make a rule that team members can't help each other.

The team that ends up making the most matches wins!

ALPHABET GREETINGS PLAYLET

As students act out this playlet, they will meet the letters of the alphabet as well as their new classmates. There are 26 parts—one for each letter of the alphabet. If you have fewer than 26 children in your class, give some students two parts each. If you have more than 26 children, give some students special roles such as director, costume helper, or prompter.

If you wish, you can have your students wear the letters they are playing. Write the letters on paper plates or sheet of paper and use string to hang them around your students' necks.

And now, on with the show!

ALL STUDENTS: We are the alphabet, and we are here
To greet all the children in our class this year.
Our letters are different, they're not the same,
But each of us is used to start someone's name!

LETTER A:　　　I'm letter A, as in Apple and Art,
Does anybody's name have A for a start?

(All students whose first names start with the letter A step forward. One by one, these students shake hands with Letter A and say: "My name is ＿＿＿＿＿ . It starts with an A." As they shake, Letter A says: "How do you do, how do you do, how do you do." The students then step back in line.)

LETTER B:　　　I'm letter B, as in Baseball and Better,
Does anybody's name have B for the first letter?

(Students whose first names start with B do the same as those whose names started with the letter A. Use this procedure throughout the course of the playlet.)

LETTER C:　　　I'm letter C, as in Cat and Cheer,
Does anybody's name start with C who is here?

LETTER D:　　　I'm letter D, as in Dog and Dance,
Does anybody's name start with D, by any chance?

LETTER E:　　　I'm letter E, as in Elephant and Egg,
If your name starts with E, step forward, I beg!

LETTER F:　　　I'm letter F, as in Fly and Flew,
If your name starts with F, I'd like to meet *you*!

LETTER G:　　　I'm letter G, as in Girl and Go,
Does your name start with G? I'd like to know!

LETTER H:　　　I'm letter H, as in Help and Hunt,
Does anybody's name have an H at the front?

LETTER I:　　　I'm letter I, as in Igloo and Ice,
If your name starts with I, I think it's nice!

LETTER J:	I'm letter J, as in Jump and Jive, If your name starts with J, I'll give you five!
LETTER K:	I'm letter K, as in Kitten and Kite. If your name starts with K, I think you're alright.
LETTER L:	I'm letter L, as in Letter and Land, If your name starts with L, come shake my hand!
LETTER M:	I'm letter M, as in Mailbox and Me, If your name starts with M, what might it be?
LETTER N:	I'm letter N, as in Noise and No, If your name starts with N, let's say hello!
LETTER O:	I'm letter O, as in Open and On, If your name starts with O, come here, don't be gone!
LETTER P:	I'm letter P, as in Pencil and Pass, Does anybody's name start with P in the class?
LETTER Q:	I'm letter Q, as in Queen and Quack, If your name starts with Q, step out, don't step back!
LETTER R:	I'm letter R, as in Rope and Red, Does anybody's name have an R at the head?
LETTER S:	I'm letter S, as in Seesaw and Sound, Does anybody's name start with S who's around?
LETTER T:	I'm letter T, as in Toy and Tie, If your name starts with T, come here, don't be shy!
LETTER U:	I'm letter U, as in Up and Umbrella, Does your name start with U, any gal, any fella'?
LETTER V:	I'm letter V, as in Voice and Violin, When you spell your name, with V does it begin?
LETTER W:	I'm letter W, as in Window and Way, If your name starts with W, let's shake hands today!
LETTER X:	I'm letter X, as in X-ray and Xylophone, Does anybody's name start with X who is known?
LETTER Y:	I'm letter Y, as in Yellow and Yam, If your name starts with Y, I'm glad to meet you, I am!
LETTER Z:	I'm letter Z, as in Zebra and Zoom, Does anybody's name start with Z in the room?
ALL STUDENTS:	We are the alphabet, and we are here To greet all the children in our class this year. Our letters are different, they're not the same, But each of us is used to start someone's name!

GETTING TO KNOW
EACH OTHER

STUDENT RAPS

Record rap songs in your classroom? It's not as difficult as it sounds! With the use of a simple tape recorder, you can turn your classroom into a recording studio.

Begin by asking students to write two-line poems that start with their names and end with something they like. Give these examples:

> "My name is Jodi, I'm okay,
>   I like to feed my fish each day."
>
> "My name is Linda, boys and girls,
>   I like to put my hair in curls."
>
> "My name is Thomas, I am tall,
>   I love to play basketball."

After students have written their couplets, it's time for them to take turns at the tape recorder. Whe you're done, play back the entire tape and enjoy your Student Raps.

STUDENT TEACHERS

All children have something to teach their classmates—whether it's how to wash the family dog, make homemade pizza, or oil a baseball mitt—and this activity gives them the opportunity to do just that.

Invite each student to give a brief "How to" presentation. It should include one or more visual aids. You may wish to give the children time to rehearse their presentations in front of one other student before speaking to the whole class. Be sure to allow time after each presentation for questions.

PERSONALITY BAGS

At the beginning of the school year it's a good idea to learn a little something about each student—and "Personality Bags" are a great way to do that!

Ask your students to bring in grocery bags with five things that tell about themselves inside. The items might be favorite toys, books, articles of clothing, and/or photos. Then have each student make a brief presentation, explaining why each item is in the bag.

A typical presentation might be:

> "This is a picture of my dog. I walk him every morning and evening. This is a can of tuna, which is my favorite kind of sandwich. This is a baby rattle, because my mother just had a baby boy. This is a marble. I won the Neighborhood Marble Championship last summer. And this is an old sneaker, because I like to play kickball."

Allow time for class questions at the end of each presentation. You may want to share your own bag with students too!

PET PRESENTATIONS

You'd be surprised at the variety of pets your students have at home. Invite them to bring in pictures of their pets, or, if possible, to bring in the pets themselves. If students have no pets, they can make one up.

Ask each student to give a brief presentation that mentions:

1. the type of pet
2. the pet's name
3. where the pet came from
4. how old it is
5. what it eats
6. what its habits are
7. what care is required

Then have students sing about their classmates' pets to the tune of "Mary Had a Little Lamb." For example, if Danny has a pet frog named Hopper, they would sing:

> Danny has a little frog,
> Little frog,
> Little frog,
> Danny has a little frog,
> And its name is Hopper!

MYSTERY WORD

What's a shebop?! That's exactly the question your students will be asking when they play this entertaining word game.

Ask each student to think of a favorite possession, such as a pet frog, a pogo stick, or a bicycle. Ask the student to write three sentences about the item, without mentioning its name. Instead, the word "shebop" should be used in its place. For example:

- I have a shebop on the table next to my bed.
- I listen to my shebop at night before going to sleep.
- I have 12 tapes to play in my shebop.

Call on a student to read his sentences aloud. See how many classmates can correctly guess what the shebop is. If no one guesses correctly, have the reader offer more clues or reveal the answer.

Continue playing until all students have participated.

HANDWRITING MATCHUP GAME

Each child in your class has distinctive handwriting. Challenge your students to note the subtleties with this enjoyable activity. Ask each student to write three sentences about himself on a slip of paper. Put these sentences on the board as examples:

1. I like to go camping.
2. I love to read adventure books.
3. My favorite cartoon character is Mighty Mouse.

Then, on another slip of paper, have each student write his name. Assign a number to each sentence slip; assign a letter to each name slip. Post the sentences on the left side of the bulletin board and the names on the right.

Now, invite your students to come up to the bulletin board, read both the sentence slips and the name slips, and try to match them up by paying careful attention to handwriting. Have your students record their answers. Can anybody get them all right?

MYSTERY CLASSMATE

After a few weeks of school, this engaging activity is a great way to reinforce what children have learned about their classmates.

Have a volunteer assume the identity of a classmate he knows well. Tell students to take turns questioning the child in an attempt to find out who the unnamed classmate is. All questions must be answerable with a "yes" or "no." For example:

> "Are you a boy?"
> "Do you like to play baseball?"
> "Are you good at arithmetic?"
> "Do you have a pet dog?"

Allow each student to ask one question. When everyone has participated, have students say who they think the "mystery person" is. Then have the child reveal the answer. Repeat the game as often as you wish, using a new volunteer each time.

WHO AM I? GUESSING GAME

In "Mystery Classmate," the class tries to discover the secret identity of a fellow student. But in this version of the game, one student tries to discover her own secret identity—revealed to everyone else!

Prepare by having each child write her name in large letters on a strip of paper about 20 inches long and 6 inches high (about 50 centimeters x 15 centimeters). Put all of them in a box. Then have one student come forward and pick a piece of paper, without looking at the name on it. Tape it around the student's head so the name appears on her forehead for the whole class to read.

The student then tries to guess whose identity is on the headband by asking only "yes" or "no" questions.

> "Am I a girl?"
> "Do I have dark hair?"
> "Do I wear glasses?"
> "Am I tall?"

Once the student thinks she knows her "secret identity," she may take a guess. If she guesses wrong three times, reveal the answer. Then call another student to wear a different headband.

GUESS WHO? WRITING EXERCISE

This writing exercise is a fun and effective way for students to get acquainted with their new classmates.

Begin by having each student write his name at the top of a piece of paper. Collect the papers and then redistribute them at random. If a child receives his own name, ask him to trade papers with a neighbor.

Since students may not know everybody's names, have each child stand up and introduce himself. Then write these five questions on the board:

1. What color are his/her eyes?
2. What color is his/her hair?
3. How tall is he/she?
4. Does he/she wear glasses?
5. What is he/she wearing today?

Tell students to answer the questions about the child whose name appears on the paper they received. Have them write their responses on that same sheet of paper.

When everyone is finished, collect the papers and choose one at random. Read the description aloud. How many classmates can guess who the subject is? Continue reading the papers aloud until every child has been described.

MYSTERY PHOTO GAME

It's easy to identify a person from his photo, but not so easy when only a fraction of that photo is revealed, as in this fun-filled activity.

Take a Polaroid picture of each child in your class. Have your students gather in a group close to you. Secretly select one photo and place it in an envelope. Very slowly, start to pull the picture from the envelope. Stop when the top of the subject's head is visible. Then ask, "Can anyone identify this person?"

If no one can guess correctly, pull a little more of the picture out of the envelope. See which student can be the first to identify his classmate. Repeat the activity using several or all of the photos.

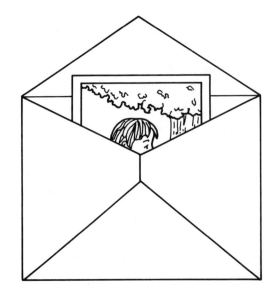

BABY PICTURE GUESSING GAME

No child likes to be called a "baby." But all children love to show their baby pictures to friends!

Ask your students to bring in pictures of themselves as babies. Display all the photos on the bulletin board, and label each one with a number. Then ask the children to guess who the babies are. Tell them to record their answers on sheets of paper, for example Baby 1 = Alexander.

When everyone is done, point to each picture on the board and ask the subject to raise his hand. See how many students guessed correctly.

SUMMER REVISITED ACTIVITIES

The first day of school, children like to talk about their summer experiences. Instead of the standard "What I Did on My Summer Vacation" composition, ask your students to try some of these activities:

1. Simulate a radio or television news broadcast called "The Summer in Review." Have your students contribute reports on their most exciting experience of the summer.

2. Choose one student to pantomime a summer adventure, such as catching a really big fish. Choose another student to try to narrate what's going on. Repeat the activity until everyone has participated.

3. Tell each child to write a description of a funny, scary, weird, or memorable person they met over the summer.

4. Have your students write thank-you notes to special people who helped them over the summer.

5. Ask each child to write and design an advertisement for a super place they visited over the summer—whether that's The Grand Canyon or Steve's Ice Cream Parlor.

SUMMER SONGFEST

Instead of having students *talk* about their summer vacations, why not have students *sing* about them? Here's how:

First, pass out paper and instruct each student to write a four-line poem about his summer vacation. Each line should be about 6 to 10 words long. Point out that the last words in lines 1 and 2 must rhyme, as well as the last words in lines 3 and 4.

Then choose a student—(Roberto, for example)—to come to the front of the class. Have your students sing the following song to the tune of "Pussycat, Pussycat":

> Roberto, Roberto, where have you been?
> Over the summer what fun were you in?
> Roberto, Roberto, what did you do?
> Tell us, Roberto, because we like you!

Have Roberto respond by singing the rhyme he wrote:

> Over the summer I went to camp,
> It rained a lot and my clothes all got damp.
> Over the summer I watched TV,
> And played with my brother who now is three!

Repeat the activity until everyone has had a chance to sing about their summer!

ACCENTUATE THE POSITIVE

It's imperative that your students feel good about their classmates. Here's a special activity to help them accentuate the positive.

After the first few weeks of school—when students have gotten the chance to know each other a bit—distribute a Positive Remarks sheet, similar to the one below. Make sure it has the names of all the children in your class on it. Ask students to think of one nice thing to say about each person on the list, and to write it next to the name.

Later, you may wish to read aloud some of the class's positive remarks.

Positive Remarks	
Ramon	He tells good jokes
Laura	She is great at spelling
Debbie	
Sam	
Melony	
Josh	
Christy	
Dominic	
Rosa	
Mike	

BIRTHDAY TIMELINE

Children won't have trouble remembering their own birthdays but they may have trouble recalling the birthdays of their classmates. You can solve this problem by creating a Birthday Timeline at the start of the year.

Give each student a sheet of white or light-colored construction paper. Tell each of your students to write their date of birth (month and day only) at the top of the paper, and underneath it their name. Then have them fill the rest of the page with a drawing. The picture might show a birthday gift they once received or would like to receive.

Collect all the papers and ask your students to help you arrange them in chronological order. String a rope across the room, and clip the papers to the rope in that order.

Now all of your students' birthdays are where everyone can see them! Each week or month, assign a birthday monitor to remind the class when someone's birthday is approaching.

LEARNING ABOUT
NEW PLACES

There's no reason why a tour of the school building can't be something to sing about! As your class approaches each important site, sing a song about it to the tune of "She'll Be Comin' Round the Mountain." For example:

> We'll be comin' to the library when we read,
> We'll be comin' to the library when we read,
> We'll be comin' to the library,
> We'll be comin' to the library,
> We'll be comin' to the library when we read!

Other verses might include:

> We'll be comin' to the lunchroom when we eat . . .
> We'll be comin' to the auditorium when we meet . . .
> We'll be comin' to the nurse when we're sick . . .
> We'll be comin' to the principal when we're late . . .
> We'll be comin' to the playground when we play . . .
> We'll be comin' to the bus stop when we leave . . .

Be sure to have your students sing softly if other classes are in session.

LETTER HUNT

Looking for a fun way to acquaint your students with their way around the school building? Why not start the year with a Letter Hunt?

To prepare, cut out cardboard letters (each about 12 inches high) that spell out a word, such as WELCOME or SEPTEMBER.

Each day before class begins, tape one of the letters on a wall somewhere in the school building. You need not display each letter in the order that it comes in the word.

Every morning, give your students a clue to help them find the day's hidden letter. For example, the first day of the activity you might say:

"Today's letter is on a wall you'll pass when you're hungry." (Hang that letter on a wall outside the cafeteria.)

On the second day of the activity you might say:

"Today's letter hangs on a wall you'll pass if you don't feel well." (Hang that letter on a wall outside the nurse's office.)

Tell the students to write down the letter they find each day. When all the letters have been displayed, challenge the students to unscramble the letters and spell the mystery word!

CLASS-CREATED SCHOOL MAP

For new students, the school building is the equivalent of a strange land. So why not create a super map to help them find their way around?

Divide the class into groups, and assign each group a different floor or area of the building to map out. Begin with a walking tour of the building. Point out all the rooms you pass and ask questions along the way to keep your students' attention focused. For example:

1. What room is between the principal's office and the gym?
2. How many classrooms are on this floor?
3. If you walk left from Room 106, which office will you come to first?

Back in the classroom, give each group of students a large sheet of butcher paper to draw their portion of the map on. They may want to draw a rough draft on small paper first. Piece together the work of each group, and place the entire school map on the wall to refer to all year long.

READING ARROWS

This unique activity not only points children in the direction of the school library, but gives them incentive to read too.

At the start of the year, duplicate a sheet with an arrow drawn on it. Inside the arrow, write the words *Title, Author,* and *Read by* on three separate lines as illustrated below.

During the year, each time a student completes a book, give him one arrow. Have him cut out the arrow, fill in the information about the book he read, and the then attach the arrow to the wall outside your classroom. Make sure the arrow is pointing in the direction of the school library.

As more and more books are read, more and more arrows will appear—eventually wending their way to the library. Besides pointing kids in the direction of the library, the arrows serve to get the entire school interested in reading.

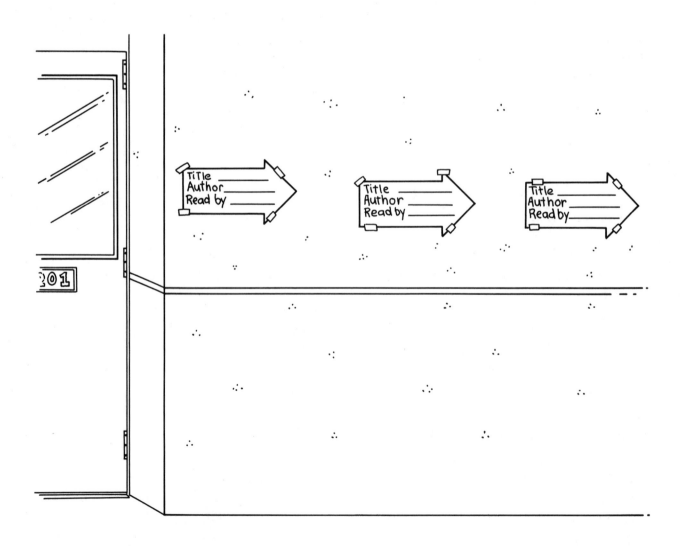

LIBRARY HUNT CARDS

Library Hunt Cards give students the impetus to explore the layout of the library and to check out books.

Make a Library Hunt Card for each child in your class. (Do this by duplicating the prototype below and pasting the copies to index cards). Distribute the cards to your class. Have each student sign her name to the card and make a checkmark next to the type of book she wishes to borrow. Now you're ready to go to the library.

Ask the librarian to explain the basic layout of the room, then let your students inspect the shelves until they each find the type of book they indicated they wanted.

Plan more "library hunts" throughout the school year! See if any students can read a book in every category.

In the library, I want to find a book about: Name _____

____ an animal   ____ a famous person

____ an athlete   ____ a family

____ a detective   ____ a holiday

____ a monster   ____ a faraway place

____ a trip to outer space   ____ a group of friends

____ an Indian   ____ a sea adventure

____ a scientist   ____ other _____
                                       (write your choice)

CLASSROOM DISCOVERIES

At the beginning of the school year, children will want to investigate all the nooks and crannies of your classroom. Why not turn this discovery period into a game?

Distribute a sheet with the following questions on it to each student. Challenge each of them to find at least one answer to every question.

---

1. Can you find something made of wood? _____

2. Can you find something made of plastic? _____

3. Can you find something made of metal? _____

4. Can you find something taller than you? _____

5. Can you find something shorter than you? _____

6. Can you find something that starts with the letter n? _____

7. Can you find something that is green? _____

8. Can you find something that has corners? _____

9. Can you find something that has wheels? _____

10. Can you find something too heavy for you to lift? _____

11. Can you find something you can see through? _____

12. Can you find something that hangs? _____

13. Can you find something that locks? _____

14. Can you find something that snaps? _____

15. Can you find something that rattles? _____

When students are done, have them share their answers with the class. You'll be amazed at the variety of items they came up with.

MYSTERY OBJECTS

If you don't know what your students are talking about—good! That's the point of this activity.

In this game, have each student secretly select an object in the classroom. Then choose a child to describe that object without saying what it is. For example, if the student selected a globe he might say: "This object is round. It spins around. Its colors are blue, pink, and green." Have your class members guess what the object is. Allow the student who guesses correctly to give the next description.

Be sure to warn students not to look at the object when they give their clues. Eye contact can be a giveaway.

ALUMNI CLASSROOM VISITS

Your new students will be very curious about what the coming year will bring. You can help give them an idea by inviting a few of last year's students to visit your classroom and talk to the new class. Former students can tell about projects and activities they especially enjoyed, and provide a number of helpful tips.

Before your former students arrive, ask the members of this year's class to prepare questions for their guests. For example:

1. Did you think last year was hard?
2. What did you like doing the most all year?
3. How did the class celebrate holidays?
4. What advice would you give us for having fun this year?

After the former students have spoken to the class, open up the session for questions and answers. Remember, there's no teacher like experience!

OUTSIDE SCOOP WALKING TOUR

At the beginning of the year, children will want to know what's *outside* the school building as well as what's inside. You can give them the outside scoop by conducting a short walking tour. While outdoors give students one or more of these challenges:

1. Find places or things outside with names that start with each different letter of the alphabet, for example: acorns, bush, Cedar Street, driveway, and so on. Have students jot down lists as they walk, or dictate the things to you.

2. Find different objects of the same color. For example, how many things can you spot that are green? Green grass and green tree leaves are a start. How many other objects can your students locate?

3. Find things that come in the same quantity. For example, how many objects do your see in threes? Are there three swings? Three doors? Three windows? Three buses?

You or your students may think of other challenges to pursue while getting the "outside scoop."

FUN WITH LEAVES

Early in the school year, use the leaves that fall from the trees for both of these classroom activities. Go outside with your students and have them collect leaves in plastic sandwich bags.

1. In the classroom, provide students with paper, crayons, glue, and scissors. Challenge your students to create pictures of people, animals, and objects using their leaves. For example, a leaf with twigs for whiskers and acorns for eyes may make an amusing cat; a leaf with a triangular bottom drawn beneath it may make an unusual sailboat.

2. Get some tree reference books from the library. Help each student to research one of his leaves. What kind of tree is it from? Then have the child place the leaf beneath a sheet of thin paper and, using a pencil or crayon, make a leaf rubbing. Tell students to write the names of their leaves under their rubbings. Hang them on a bulletin board.

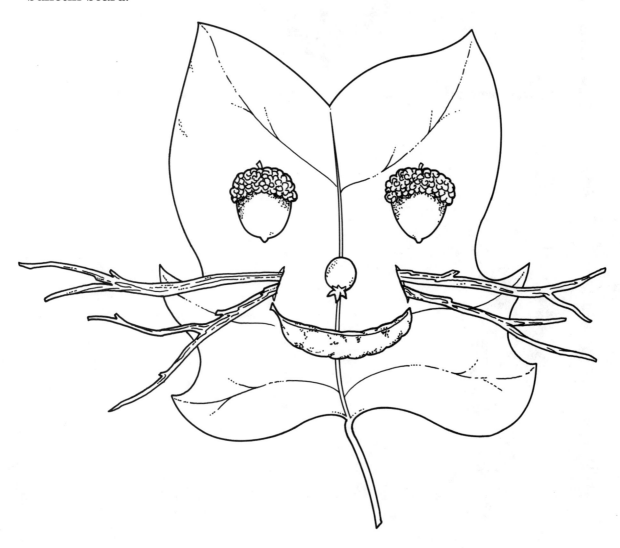

FUN FOR THE WHOLE CLASS

CLASS-PRIDE CREATIONS

Every state has its own state flag, state bird, state flower, state tree, state motto, and state seal. And your class can too!

Using an encyclopedia, show kids their state's flag, etc. Discuss why their state has these special things. Point out that the special things help make the state a little different from the rest, and make everyone in the state proud. Likewise, your students can develop class pride by designating each of the following:

- a class flag or seal
- a class motto
- a class song
- a class bird
- a class tree
- a class flower

Break the class into committees for each category. Encourage as much originality as possible. For example, each child in the Class Tree Committee can design his own class tree rather than choosing a tree that already exists, each child on the Class Song Committee can write new lyrics to a popular song rather than use the original version.

When all the students have finished their creations, let the whole class vote on their choice for each category. Make a bulletin board display of the winners in each category.

CAREER-DAY FASHION SHOW

Unless your students are members of the royal family, it's probably too early to tell what kinds of jobs they'll hold later in life. But since school starts close to Labor Day, why not devote some September class time to learning about careers?

Have each student choose a job, find out a little about it, and prepare an appropriate costume. The jobs can include:

- sailor
- doctor
- flight attendant
- construction worker
- train engineer
- baseball player
- pilot
- dancer
- farmer
- cowboy/cowgirl
- firefighter
- police officer
- forest ranger
- nurse

On a designated Career Day, give the students the opportunity to model their outfits. (A little music in the background adds a nice touch!) After the fashion show, have the students explain what people who hold their jobs do.

As an additional activity, invite parents to come to class and speak about their careers. Have them explain the work they do and the skills that are needed to get the job done. Leave plenty of time for a question-and-answer session afterwards.

GIANT CLASSROOM CALENDAR

A Giant Classroom Calendar is the perfect way for your students to keep track of the many important events of the year.

Discuss what a calendar is and why it is useful. On a large sheet of butcher paper, draw a one-month calendar. Do not write the name of the month, days of the week, or dates—your students will do that. Then divide your class into three committees:

1. *Names and Numbers Committee:* This group uses colorful markers to fill in the month's name, days of the week, and dates. Have students write the correct date in the upper left-hand corner of each box. They may need your help to determine where each date should go.

2. *Research Committee:* This group uses almanacs and encyclopedias to find out the special days of the month. For example, September's holidays include:

   - Labor Day: first Monday
   - National Grandparent's Day: Sunday following Labor Day
   - Native American Day: fourth Friday
   - Rosh Hashannah (Jewish New Year): date varies
   - National Hispanic Week: week starting with the second Sunday

   This group also finds out which children have birthdays in the month, and if there are any class trips and assemblies scheduled. When they have completed the research, ask them to write the events in the appropriate date boxes.

3. *Decoration Committee:* This group draws pictures to illustrate the special events that the research committee finds. Tell them to make the pictures small enough to fit in the date boxes. When they are finished, paste the pictures inside the appropriate date boxes.

Refer to the classroom calendar every day. Create a new one each month.

CLASS TIMELINE

In Personal Timelines (p. 000), a timeline was used to chart the events in a student's life. But a timeline can also be used to chart the events of the class' school year.

Begin by placing a long sheet of butcher paper, perhaps six or eight feet long, on the wall. Draw a horizontal line through the middle, and then draw vertical marks to indicate each month of the school year.

Tell your students to enter information such as classmates' birthdays, field trips, upcoming units of study, and holidays on the time line. (You may have to help them determine exactly where the marks should go.) As with the personal timelines, students may draw pictures to accompany the notations.

Timelines can also be used effectively for social studies—each vertical mark indicating a different decade or century in history.

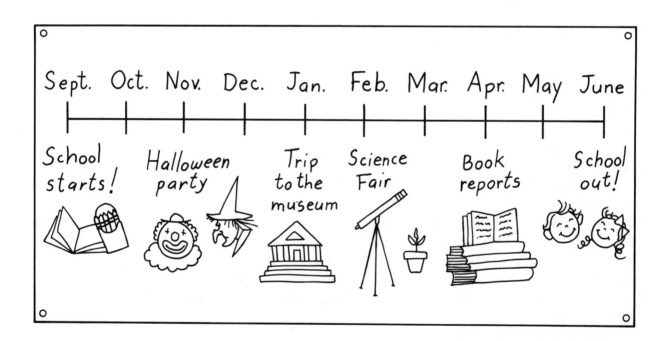

CLASS NEWSPAPER

Extra! Extra! Read all about it! New students publish their own newspaper! What better way to unite your students than with a class newspaper?

Newspaper staff positions include:

A **news reporter** writes about important events happening in school such as assemblies, class projects, or new school rules.

A **feature story writer** reports on new teachers, or students with interesting backgrounds.

An **editorial writer** gives opinions about school issues such as the cafeteria menu, playground equipment, or holiday schedules.

A **sports reporter** gives scores of games played in or outside of school.

A **movie reviewer** gives opinions about recent movies.

A **TV reviewer** reports on recent TV shows.

A **book reviewer** reports on books she has read or books that are new to the library.

A **weather reporter** writes about the temperature on recent days and offers a forecast for the future.

A **travel columnist** writes about her own or her classmates' favorite places to visit.

A **horoscope writer** predicts the future for people born at different times of the year.

A **cartoonist** draws a comic strip that tells about school experiences.

A **classified ad editor** collects ads from classmates who wish to trade or give away baseball cards, stickers, puppies, etc.

An **advertising manager** makes up ads to go in the newspaper, or creates large ads on oaktag to inform other classes about the paper.

A **distribution manager** helps run off copies of the paper and delivers them to other classes, the principal, and the librarian.

Get your students started by giving them copies of real newspapers to look at. Discuss how the articles are written and laid out on the pages. Have the class think of a great name for their classroom paper. Then assign each student a staff position.

After students have completed their stories, ads, and cartoons, it's time to put the newspaper together. To do this, you can either have the children recopy their contributions onto ditto masters or paste them onto photocopy paper. Make copies of the newspaper and distribute it to your class or the whole school.

CLASS SINGDOWN

At the start of the year, you may be wondering just how many songs your students know. Hold a Singdown and you'll find out!

To have a Singdown, divide the class into two, three, or four teams. Then announce the Singdown's theme, such as "Songs That Name a Color." Allow teams a minute or two to think of songs that contain colors. For example, this category would include: "Mary had a little lamp whose fleece was *white* as snow." "Four and twenty *black*birds baked in a pie," "And the rockets' *red* glare." Tell each team to write down the songs so they don't forget them.

When time is up, have Team A sing a song that mentions a color. Then have Team B sing a song, and so on. Continue the round until a team is eliminated because it failed to think of a song, or if it accidentally repeats a song. The last remaining team wins the round.

Start a second round with a different category, such as one of the following:

songs with a boy's name	songs naming an animal
songs with a girl's name	songs naming a day or month
songs with a number	songs that contain the word *love*
songs with the words *big* or *little*	songs naming a food

Play as many round as you wish!

CLASS RHYMEDOWN

    If your class is not in a singing mood, they're probably in a rhyming mood. So why not hold a Rhymedown?

    A Rhymedown is similar to a Singdown, except that teams must come up with rhyming words instead of song lyrics. For example, if the category were "Words That Rhyme with Cheese," one team might say, "Please." The next team might say, "Sneeze." Other words to follow might include "breeze," "trees," and "freeze." (Nonsense words are not acceptable.) A team is eliminated from the round if it fails to think of a new rhyme, or if it accidentally repeats a rhyme.

    There are endless categories you can provide for this game. Simply announce, "The category is words that rhyme with ＿＿＿＿," and use any of the words below.

face	car	cheese	nice
back	chair	meet	quick
add	art	bed	hide
grade	cat	bee	bill
bag	late	near	pin
mail	gave	bell	nine
rain	saw	ten	pink
lake	ball	end	might
came	day	her	joke
pan	week	yes	tone
hand	dream	bet	broom
lap	clean	blue	chop
for	nose	dot	sound
low	boy	rough	sum
done	cup	day	mile

PASS THE STORY, PLEASE!

Try this add-on story activity! Begin by writing the first sentence of a story on a sheet of notebook paper. For example:

Once upon a time, two birds named Toby and Lily were building a nest together, when a strong wind began to blow.

Pass the paper to the student nearest you in the classroom. Instruct her to read the sentence and then add another sentence to the story. Then have that student pass the story to her neighbor, who adds another sentence, and so on. Caution students not to finish the story until it reaches the last person in the room, who then provides an ending.

When the story is completed, read it aloud to the class.

WHO'S THE LEADER?

Here's a great way to let every student lead.

Have your children stand in a circle, and ask one to leave the room. While that student is out, designate a group leader. Tell your students to follow whatever movements the group leader makes. Movements may include clapping hands, bobbing the head, wagging the tongue, or patting the head.

Now ask the absent student to return to the classroom and stand in the middle of the circle. Have the group leader make a movement, while the others imitate it. Every 15 seconds or so, the leader should begin a new movement. Have the student in the middle try to guess who the leader is. If that student fails to identify the leader after three guesses, reveal the answer. Then play another round with a different leader and guesser.

OBSERVATION GAME

Here's an enjoyable, back-to-school activity that's guaranteed to develop your students' powers of observation.

Put the following puzzle on the chalkboard:

A   EF HI KLMN   T VWXY

   BCD   G   J   OPQRS U

Point out that each letter of the alphabet, except Z, is either above or below the line. Can anyone figure out why the letters have been separated the way they are? If no one can guess, then give your students this clue: The placement of each letter has to do with its shape. Do they see it now? The letters above the line are made with only straight lines; the letters below the line have curves. So where would Z go? Above the line, of course.

Now, think of an interesting way to divide your students into two groups. For example:

- children wearing sneakers/kids not wearing sneakers
- children with light hair/kids with dark hair
- children wearing something red/kids not wearing anything red
- children wearing a wristwatch/kids not wearing a wristwatch
- children whose first names start with A–M/kids with first names starting N–Z

Separate your students into their two groups, but don't tell them the reason. Have the two groups face each other. See who is the first to figure out the difference between them. You might find it necessary to give clues such as: "It has something to do with your shoes."

After a few rounds, challenge students to lead the activity.

HUMAN-SPELLING EXERCISE

How can you turn an ordinary spelling lesson into an exciting and unusual game? Simply by making your students the letters! That's right—Human Spelling!

Write each letter of the alphabet on a separate paper plate. Distribute a plate to each member of the class. If you have more than 26 students, assign some students special jobs such as Word Caller, Time Keeper, or Word Checker. If you have fewer than 26 students, give some students a second plate with a less-frequently used letter such as Q, X, and Z.

Ask the class to line up shoulder to shoulder and to hold their letters against their chests. Call out a word you wish spelled, such as *house.* The students holding the letters in the word—H, O, U, S, and E—should step forward about 10 feet, turn around so they are now facing their classmates, and then arrange themselves to spell the word correctly. (Younger kids may require your coaching.) You or the Time Keeper can tell the class how long it took to spell the word; You or the Word Checker can check the spelling of the word in a dictionary.

If a word contains two of the same letters, as in *baby,* ask the student holding the B to wave it back and forth in front of the person holding the A, to indicate the two places where the letter B belongs. (If this becomes too challenging for your students, limit your spelling list to words that use each letter only once.)

You may hold contests to see which group of students is the fastest at spelling 2-letter words, 3-letter words, 4-letter words, 5-letter words, and so on.

NAME THAT NOISE

Looking for an activity that's so quiet you can hear a pin drop? Try this one.

Have the entire class put their heads down on their desks and close their eyes. Tell them they must remain quiet and listen carefully. Then make one of these classroom noises:

closing a book
turning the pages of a book
using chalk on the board
closing a door
opening a window

dropping a pencil
unzipping a bookbag
snapping a lunchbox shut
switching off a light
shuffling cards

After you've made the noise, have your students try to identify it. Invite the child who guessed correctly to make the next noise. Play as many times as you wish.

RHYTHM NAME GAME

Here's a challenging activity that will hold every child's attention and teach them their classmates names too.

Make name tags for your students, or have them make their own. Tell the children to sit in a circle. Then designate a Leader for the first round. Ask her to sit in the middle of the circle.

The object of the exercise is to have students whose names are called respond without breaking the rhythm of the activity. Responses go like this:

EVERYONE: 1, 2, 3, and a zing, zing, zing.
LEADER: Terry.
TERRY: Who, me?
LEADER: Yes, you.
TERRY: Couldn't be.
LEADER: Then who?
Terry arbitrarily picks another student's name.
TERRY: Justin
JUSTIN: Who, me?
LEADER: Yes, you.
JUSTIN: Couldn't be.
LEADER: Then who?
JUSTIN: Laureen
(and so on)

If someone fails to respond correctly, then she is out. The last student left in the game wins and becomes the leader for the next round.

HANDS ACROSS THE CLASSROOM

It's always nice to have students who will give you a hand when you need it. In this activity, they'll be giving you *both* hands.

Have students trace both of their hands on sheets of construction paper. Ask them to write their first name on the left hand and their last name on the right hand. Then have them carefully cut out the hands.

With all of the student names facing in one direction, make a string of hands by taping them together—thumb to thumb on one side and little finger to little finger on the other. Hang the hands across a classroom wall. Add a banner that reads "Hands Across the Classroom" or "I Wanna' Hold Your Hand."

Use your new display to prompt a discussion on ways students can "lend each other a hand" in class this year.

There's a very good chance that at least one of your students will celebrate his birthday each month. Why not make it a class celebration? One day a month, set aside a little time to mark these happy occasions. How should you celebrate? Here's a few possibilities:

1. Have the class make a colorful cake out of construction paper, papier-maché, clay, or other materials. (A real cake is gone after it's eaten, but this one lasts forever!) Students can sign their names on rolled-up paper sticks that serve as candles.

2. Have children draw a giant birthday cake on the board with colored chalk. When it's time to blow out the candles, tell the birthday honorees to make a wish and erase the flames!

3. Have students create individual teeny-tiny birthday cards bearing teeny-tiny drawings and teeny-tiny written messages. Collect the cards and present them in a teeny-tiny envelope.

4. Have the class or individual students design an accordian card. Do this by folding a long sheet of butcher paper into dozens of sections. Write or draw a funny birthday story on the pages of the pleated paper.

5. Ask the birthday honorees to bring in baby pictures of themselves. Have each child show her photo to the class and describe what it was like being a baby!

6. Present birthday honorees with plastic cups that have their names painted on them. They can use the cups to store some of their school supplies. Other gifts might include a T-shirt, a giant papier-maché baseball, or even an old white sneaker with every classmate's signature on it.

7. Allow birthday honorees to wear a special birthday hat made by the class. It might be in the shape of a birthday cake or a gift-wrapped box with a large bow on top. Honorees can wear the hat for part or all of the day.

8. Invite the class to write special lyrics to "Happy Birthday" or another song, tailored to the honoree's personality.

   For example:
   Happy birthday to Bob,
   Happy birthday to Bob,
   In class you are friendly,
   And you do a good job!

9. Have students research the date of birth of the honoree to discover what notable events occurred on that day. Then have the class create a newspaper's front page containing headlines or short articles about those historic events. Present the newspaper to the birthday student.

Students whose birthdays fall during non-school months get a separate party, perhaps on the last week of school.

Oh, and don't forget to invite parents to join in the party fun!

GREAT BOOKS FOR THE NEW YEAR

Children start a new school year with many worries and concerns: What will my teacher be like? Will I make new friends in class? Will I find my way?

A great way to help your children make the transition from home to school is by reading good books together. Books can show your students that other people share the same worries and concerns about managing in school as they do. Books in class are an effective way to stimulate group discussions about the things on your children's minds.

Each of the following books deals in some way with children in school. At the K-2 level, you may wish to read the stories aloud to the whole class. For grades 3-5, you may want to read the stories aloud, or have children read them independently or to each other.

K-2
The Best Teacher in the World by Bernice Chardiet. Scholastic, 1990.
Did You Carry the Flag Today, Charley? by Rebecca Caudill. Illustrated by Nancy
    Grossman. Henry Holt, 1966.
Leo the Late Bloomer by Robert Kraus. Harper-Junior, 1987.
Miss Nelson Is Missing by Harry Allard. Illustrated by James Marshall. Houghton
    Mifflin, 1977.
My Teacher Sleeps in School by Leattie Weiss. Illustrated by Ellen Weiss. Puffin, 1985.
Starring First Grade by Miriam Cohen. Greenwillow, 1985.
Teach Us, Amelia Bedelia by Peggy Parish. Greenwillow, 1977.
What Mary Jo Shared by Janice May Udry. Scholastic, 1970.
When Will I Read? by Miriam Cohen. Illustrated by Lilian Hoban. Dell, 1987.
Will I Have a Friend? by Miriam Cohen. Illustrated by Lilian Hoban. Macmillan, 1967.

Grades 3–4
Cosmic Cousins by Nancy Hayashi. Dutton, 1988.
The Flunking of Joshua T. Bates by Susan Shreve. Scholastic, 1985.
In the Year of the Boar and Jackie Robinson by Bette Bao Lord. Harper-Junior, 1984.
Ramona Quimbly, Age Eight by Beverly Cleary. Dell, 1982.
The Secret Language by Ursula Nordstrom. Harper-Junior, 1960.
Tales of a Fourth Grade Nothing by Judy Blume. Dell, 1972.
Teacher's Pet by Johanna Hurwitz. Scholastic, 1989.

Grade 5
The Empty Schoolhouse by Natalie Savage Carlson. Harper-Junior, 1965.
Harriet the Spy by Louise Fitzhugh. Harper-Junior, 1964.
Homesick: My Own Story by Jean Fritz. Dell, 1982.
Maggie Marmelstein for President by Marjorie Weinman Sharmat. Harper-Junior, 1975.
Nothing's Fair in Fifth Grade by Barthe DeClements. Puffin, 1990.
Nutty for President by Dean Hughes. Bantam, 1986.
Philip Hall Likes Me, I Reckon Maybe by Bette Greene. Dial, 1974.
Sixth Grade Can Really Kill You by Barthe DeClements. Scholastic, 1986.

SUPER CLASS YEARBOOK

You probably associate a yearbook with the end of the school year. But there's no time like the present to start planning for it!

A Class Yearbook should contain a wide variety of student writing.

Throughout the year, have students write briefly on these and other topics:

1. A school event that made me happy (or sad)
2. The greatest field trip ever
3. The hardest I ever laughed in school
4. My favorite school lunch
5. The most exciting game this year
6. The biggest surprise of the year
7. My favorite school holiday
8. Why I like my classroom

Encourage them to draw pictures to accompany their writing. By the end of the year, you'll have more than enough material to publish a Super Class Yearbook!

PARTNER AND
SMALL-GROUP ACTIVITIES

MYSTERY BAG

Your new students may take their sense of touch for granted. But this enjoyable game is sure to change that.

Divide your class into small groups. Give each group a paper bag filled with a variety of objects such as an eraser, a paperclip, a leaf, a small mirror, and a marble. Have one student from the group stick his hand into the bag and, without looking, pick an object and hold it inside the bag. Ask the student to describe how it feels. For example, is it smooth, sharp, heavy, or squishy? Then have everybody in the group, including that student, attempt to guess what the object is. When the group is done guessing, remove the object from the bag and see who was correct.

Follow the same procedure, until everyone has had an opportunity to feel an object.

MATCHMAKER GAME

At the start of the school year, making new friends will be on everyone's agenda. This super activity is guaranteed to help your students do just that.

Before class, find several large magazine photos and cut each of them in half. Make sure you have enough to give each student half a picture. Mix up the photo halves and give one to each child. (If you have an odd number of children, you can take a photo half yourself!)

Challenge your class to mingle until each student finds the classmate with the other half of his picture. Then instruct the partners to talk with one another until they discover at least three things they have in common—anything from hair color to favorite food will do. Also, have them find out three ways they are different.

Later, invite each pair of students to stand before the class. Tell them to display their whole magazine picture, and list the ways they are like and unlike their partner.

PARTNER PRINTS

Begin this activity by asking your students why they think the police copy the fingerprints of people they arrest. Explain that no two sets of fingerprints are exactly alike. Therefore, they make a good means of identification.

Now, have each of your children make copies of their own fingerprints, using an inkpad and a sheet of white paper. Ask them to write their names under their prints.

Then pair off students. Tell them to carefully compare their own prints with those of their partner. How many differences can they detect.

Later, display all prints on the bulletin board under the heading: Each of Us Is Unique!

INVENT A HOLIDAY

There's no doubt that your new students love holidays. So why not invite them to invent their own?

Begin by dividing students into small groups and asking them this question: "What *new* holiday would you like to invent for the coming year?" The holiday can be silly, like National Upside-Down Day or meaningful, like Give Thanks to Safety Patrol Day.

Tell groups to think about these questions when creating their holiday:

1. What is the name of your holiday?
2. On what day of the year does it occur?
3. What, exactly, does the holiday celebrate or remember?
4. How should people observe the holiday?

Have each group write a short paragraph that tells about its holiday. Then have them design a special flag or stamp to commemorate it. They can also write a holiday song or poem.

Hold a Holiday Celebration in your classroom. Invite each group to share its work with the class. Add to the festivities with a special holiday parade or feast. Finally, post all the writing and drawings on a bulletin board entitled Our Special Holidays.

PARTNER PRESENTS

Children love giving and getting gifts. Here's a special activity that allows them to do both—and make a new friend in the process.

Randomly assign each student a partner. Tell students to talk to their partners and to learn about their special interests, hobbies, and talents. Then challenge each student to create the perfect gift for his partner. The gift might be in the form of a picture, collage, mobile, or diorama. A baseball enthusiast, for example, might enjoy receiving a collage of baseball scenes taken from sports magazines. A fledgling magician might like to get a rabbit made from a stuffed sock.

When all students have completed making their gifts, have them share them with the class and explain why the gift is so perfect for their partner.

ME AND MY SHADOW ARTS-AND-CRAFTS

At the start of the school year, you'll want complete profiles on every student. Here's a creative way to get them: Have your children pair off and make shadow portraits!

It is best to do this activity when the sun is either high or low in the sky. Instruct each student to take a sheet of white paper. If it is early morning or late afternoon, tape the paper to the wall. If it's around noon, tape it to the floor. Either way, make sure the paper is positioned so that the student's shadow falls on it when she stands nearby. Then tell the partners to take turns tracing each other's shadows with a pencil or marker.

When both profiles are complete, tell students to cut them out and paste them on pieces of black construction paper. Hang the results on a classroom wall under the heading Silhouette Gallery.

As an additional activity, see if students can identify the model for each silhouette.

SHAPE ART

This unique partner activity teaches children about shapes while stimulating their creativity.

On a sheet of paper, draw several different shapes of various sizes. Be sure to include plenty of squares, rectangles, circles, and triangles. Duplicate a copy for each student in class. Then have your students pair off and cut out their shapes. Challenge the partners to see how many different designs they can make by arranging and rearranging the shapes.

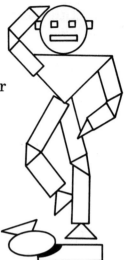

After each set of partners has created their favorite design, have them paste it on construction paper and then color it. Later, have each set of partners come to the front of the class, display their work, and describe it to classmates. Encourage creative descriptions such as, "This is a dancing robot," or "This is a skyscraper on wheels." You'll be amazed by what they come up with.

OPPOSITES ATTRACT ACTIVITY

Opposites will attract in this lively activity designed to help new students get acquainted.

On separate index cards, write each of the following words:

hot	fast	happy	new
cold	slow	sad	old
short	near	noisy	good
tall	far	quiet	bad
nice	neat	hard	dim
mean	messy	soft	bright

Shuffle the cards and have each student pick one. (If you have more than 24 students, you'll have to provide a few more opposites.

Now have the students mingle until they each find their opposite partners.

Tell students who are paired off to search through magazines for pictures that relate to the words on their cards. For example, if their cards say "hot" and "cold," pictures of the desert and Alaska would be appropriate. Have them cut out as many pictures as they can find, and paste them on sheets of oaktag or construction paper. At the top of the paper, they should write their two opposite words.

When all work is complete, display the pictures on a bulletin board called Opposites Attract.

GUESS WORD

At the start of the school year you'll want to get an idea of how strong your students' language skills are. A simple game of Guess Word will give you the answer.

Gather 50 or so index cards. On each card write one word your students are familiar with, such as:

school	happy	birthday
baseball	brother	circus
kitchen	telephone	animal
cereal	penny	roar
rain	surprise	quiet

Have students pair off and play two against two. Distribute a few cards to each of them. Instruct one player on each team to read the word on the first card, without letting his partner see it. Have the player on Team A give a one-word hint to his partner, who then tries to guess the word on the card. For example, if the word were *telephone*, the player might say, "Talk" or "Dial."

If the partner guesses the word, Team A gets 5 points, and a new word is given. If the partner fails to guess the word, then a player on Team B gives another one-word hint to his partner, who tries to guess the word for 4 points. The value of the word decreases by one point with every new hint. If neither team has guessed the word after five tries, the word is revealed to both sides and discarded.

Have players alternate as the hint-givers and hint-receivers. When each team has used all of its cards, have them trade cards with distantly stationed classmates.

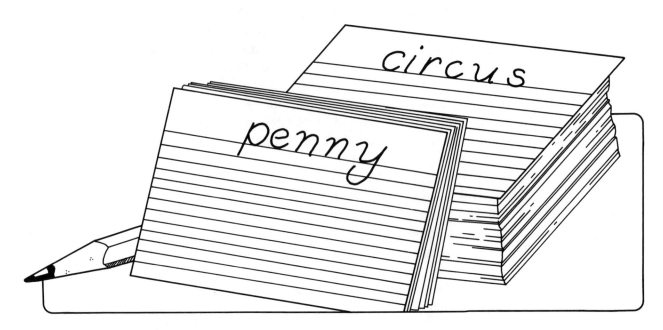

PARTNER HEADLINES

If your students ever dreamed of seeing their names in print, now's their chance!

Have students pair off with classmates. Ask each student to write his name neatly on a piece of paper and give it to his partner. Then have students print their partners' names by cutting out letters from newspaper or magazine headlines, and pasting them on construction paper. When everyone's done, each student will have his own name in print.

As an additional challenge, have students cut out letters to form positive headlines about their partners. For example:

> Lisa Thomas has a great smile
> Bernie Grey is a math whiz
> Laureen Harris is a wonderful friend

Display the printed names and headlines prominently in the classroom. That way, your new students will become familiar with their classmates names.

PICTURE TALES

Begin by tearing out dozens of magazine pictures. The pictures can be of anything—from a snow-covered house to a famous actress. Divide the class into small groups, and distribute five pictures to each of them. Challenge the groups to invent stories based on the pictures, which they can arrange in any order.

After students decide on a story, have them paste the pictures, in the appropriate order, on a large sheet of oaktag. Instruct them to write one or two sentences under each picture to explain what is happening in that part of the story.

When all groups are done, ask them to share their pictures and stories with the rest of the class.

What will the future year bring for your class? Why not let your students guess!

Pair off students, and ask them to tell their partners several things about themselves such as their favorite sports, hobbies, and books. Then based on what they have learned, have each student make three predictions about his partner. Those predictions might be:

1. In the coming year, your dog will have four puppies.
2. In the coming year, you will collect 100 new stickers.
3. In the coming year, your Little League team will win seven games.

Have students record their predictions and place them in a designated box. Store the box out of sight. At the end of the year, tell students to reread their predictions and see how many came true.

ILLUSTRATED INITIALS

Tap into your new students' artistic abilities with this great quiet-time activity.

Tell each student to write her initials in big letters on a sheet of white paper. Then tell the student to use the initials to create a picture or design. For example, the letter "U" can serve as the bottom of a boat; the letter "M" can be mountain peaks or the ears on a cat.

When kids are done, have them trade papers with a partner. Can each partner find the initials?

STORY PANTOMIME

Start the school year *quietly* with this enjoyable pantomime activity.

Choose a story to read aloud to your students. Then select some students to come forward and pantomime the actions of the characters as you read. Choose one child for each role. If the story is long, you may wish to substitute the cast with new class members.

In a related activity, have a group of students silently act out a story for the rest of the class. Later, challenge the audience to guess which story was performed.

PAPER-BAG DRAMATICS

Make the start of school *dramatic* with this exciting activity.

Divide your class into groups, provide each group with a large paper bag filled with a variety of objects such as:

- an old sock
- a ruler
- a paper cup
- a leaf
- a rubber ball
- a pencil

You may put the same items in each bag, or make each bag different.

Give the groups about ten minutes to prepare short skits that somehow use all of the objects in their bags as props. Urge each group to be as creative as possible. For example, a student holding a leaf could be a tree, or a child holding a paper cup over his nose could be a pig.

When all groups are ready, have them perform their skits for the class.

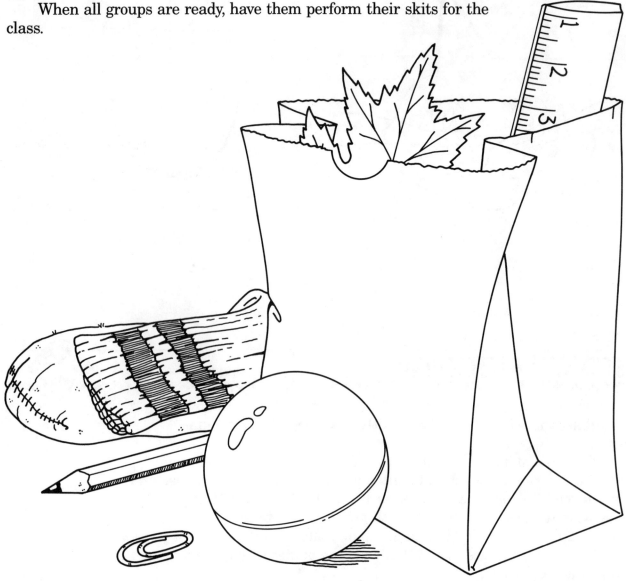

WORD-BY-WORD STORIES

Here's a creative exercise guaranteed to hold every child's attention.

Divide students into pairs or groups. Ask one child in each group to start a story by saying its first word. Then have other students in the group take turns adding words until sentences—and eventually stories—are formed. For example:

Student #1: Once
Student #2: upon
Student #3: a
Student #4: time

Student #5: there
Student #6: lived
Student #7: a
Student #8: prince.

You'll be surprised at the wild twists and turns a Word-by-Word Story can take!

CARD ARITHMETIC

This simple activity helps your new students brush up on their math skills.

Before you begin, you'll need to get ahold of several decks of playing cards. (If you can't, make your own from index cards.) Divide children into pairs and give each pair a deck of cards. Tell them to remove the picture cards, which won't be needed.

Have one student shuffle the deck and turn over two cards. The first student in the pair to call out the correct sum of the two numbers wins the round and gets a point. Then two more cards are turned over and so on. More advanced players can add three, four, or five cards. When all cards are used up, instruct students to reshuffle their decks. At the end of the game, the student who has the most points wins.

This game can also be used for subtraction. After two cards have been turned over, tell students to subtract the lower number from the higher number.

INDIVIDUAL STUDENT
ACTIVITIES

BEFORE AND AFTER

Over the course of the school year, your students will change a lot. This activity gives them the unique opportunity to measure—at least some of—that change.

Duplicate the measurement sheet below and distribute one to each student. Tell them to fill in the information requested in the left column.

Provide a scale for kids to weigh themselves on and a height chart to indicate how tall they are. Have students measure their ankles, knees, wrists, and waists, by wrapping a piece of string around each body part, and then measuring the length of the string.

Name _____

Beginning of school	End of school
_____ inches (centimeters) tall	_____
_____ pounds (grams)	_____
_____ ankles (in inches or centimeters around)	_____
_____ knees	_____
_____ wrists	_____
_____ waist	_____
_____ shoe size	_____
_____ shirt or dress size	_____

Once they are filled out, collect the sheets and store them until the end of the year. Then redistribute them, and have students fill them in again. Discuss the ways in which children have changed the most.

PORTRAIT POEMS

If you're hunting for a quiet-time activity that combines art and writing than Portrait Poems are for you.

First, have each student draw a self-portrait and paste it on the top half of a sheet of construction paper. Then have the student write an acrostic poem, using the letters of her first name, to describe herself. For example:

J jacks champion
A active
C careful
K kids around a lot
I ice cream lover
E eight years old

Tell students to paste their poems beneath their portraits. Display the results on a class bulletin board. Invite the class to circulate in the portrait gallery and enjoy each other's art work and writing.

STUDENT COATS OF ARMS

Ask students if they know what a coat of arms is. Explain that it is a special design created to represent an important family. Coats of arms were first used in the 1100s to help knights be recognized on the battlefield. The coat of arms usually appeared on a knight's shield.

Although your students aren't knights, they can still enjoy making their own coat of arms. Duplicate the shield below and distribute a copy to each student. Give them the following directions:

1. In the upper-left box, write your full name.
2. In the upper-right box, draw a picture of yourself.
3. In the lower-left box, draw a picture of your favorite activity.
4. In the lower-right box, draw a picture of your home or room.

When students are finished, they'll have their own coats of arms. Display all work on the bulletin board under the heading "Class Coats of Arms."

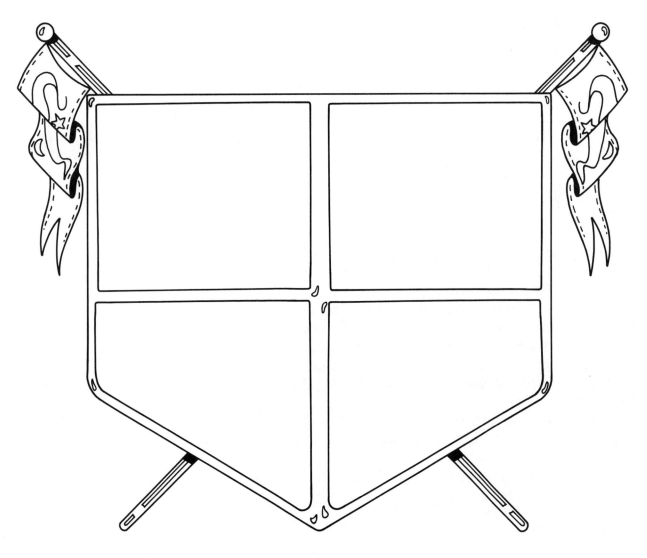

IN-THE-BAG GUESSING GAME

Children love to solve mysteries. Here's one that's literally in the bag.

Ask each student to bring a mystery object to class in a paper bag. Then invite a child to step forward and answer questions about what's in her bag. Each must be answerable with a "yes" or "no." Questions might be as follows:

> "Is your object used for writing?"
> "Does it come in different sizes?"
> "Is it made of wood?"
> "Will it break if you drop it?"
> "Does it have any kind of smell?"
> "Does it feel fuzzy?"

Allow each student in class to ask one question, and then have them guess what object is in the bag. A student who guesses correctly can be the next to bring her bag to the front of the class.

TRASH INVENTIONS

Start the school year with a pile of junk? That exactly what your class does in this stimulating activity.

Ask your students to bring to class any trash or garbage lying around at home, such as empty egg cartons, milk containers, juice cans, food boxes, toilet paper tubes, plastic butter tubs, string, rubber bands, paper wrappers—you name it!

Challenge your students to make practical or wacky inventions from their junk. For example, one kid might decorate a juice can and use it to hold his school supplies. Another might attach several toilet paper tubes end to end to create a class telescope. How about a skateboard for the pet rabbit? A fall jacket for the doorknob? No idea is too wacky or weird!

When students are ready, have them present each invention to the class, explaining what its purpose is and how it was made. Take a class vote to see which invention deserves the Trash Invention Trophy—which can also be made out of trash!

ALPHABET HUNT

 Your students may be too young to read articles in the local newspaper, but reading the individual letters is as easy as ABC!
 Give each student a page from a magazine or newspaper, and challenge them to find capital and lower case versions of each letter of the alphabet.
 Duplicate the chart below and distribute one to each student. Tell children that each time they find a capital or small letter in the magazine or newspaper, they should circle it and then write that letter in the appropriate place on their chart. Can anyone find a capital and small version of all 26 letters of the alphabet?

A	a	N	n
B	b	O	o
C	c	P	p
D	d	Q	q
E	e	R	r
F	f	S	s
G	g	T	t
H	h	U	u
I	i	V	v
J	j	W	w
K	k	X	x
L	l	Y	y
M	m	Z	z

EGG CARTON COMPUTERS

At the start of the year, you'll probably want to review your students' math skills and here's an activity you can count on.

Give every child two egg cartons. In the cups of the first, have them write the numbers 1 through 12. In the cups of the second, have them write alternating + and − signs. (If your students are more advanced, have them add × and ÷ signs.) Pass out three buttons to each student.

Now kids are ready to compute. Have them stand about three feet (or 1 meter) from the egg cartons. Tell them to toss two buttons in the number carton and one button in the symbol carton. Then have children compute a math problem based on where the buttons land. For example, if their first two buttons landed on 4 and 10, and the third button landed on +, they would add 4 + 10 to get 14. If their third button landed on −, they would subtract 10 − 4 to get 6.

Challenge students to complete as many math problems as they can. Save the cartons to use again.

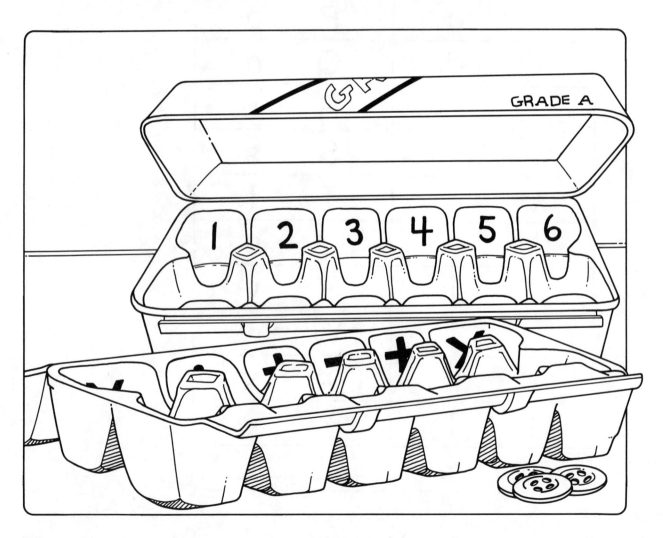

DO YOU REMEMBER?

Here's a quiet-time activity designed to entertain new students and tell you something about them.

Duplicate the following sheet of questions and distribute them to your class. Tell students to try to answer all the questions. When they're done collect their papers. You'll be surprised what you learn.

1. What was the last movie you saw? _____

2. What was the first sentence you spoke after waking up this morning? _____ _____

3. When was the last time you ate a banana? _____

4. Where were you last Sunday night at six o'clock? _____

5. What is the earliest moment in your life that you can remember? _____ _____

6. What was the first book you ever read by yourself? _____

7. Who was your first best friend? _____

8. When was the last time you laughed out loud? _____

9. When was the last time you dressed in a raincoat? _____

10. What was the first birthday party you ever went to, besides your own? _____ _____

SILLY POEMS

Students of all ages love to be silly. That's why your students will delight in creating silly poems.

A silly poem is simply a nonsense rhyming couplet. Tell your children to think of two words they want to rhyme and then write their poem. For example, the rhyming words *car* and *star* might produce this silly poem:

> I drove away in my brand-new car;
> It went so fast I parked on a star.

Silly, right? But that's the point! Invite your students to think of two words that rhyme and create their own silly poems from them. Needless to say, the sillier the better! Later, you'll have more than enough children clamoring to share their creations with the class!

WHERE HAS THE TIME GONE?

The first days of school may pass so quickly that you'll be asking, "Where did the time go?" Your students will be wondering the same thing in this game designed to sharpen their listening skills.

Begin by having a pair of volunteers leave the room. Then hide a ticking alarm clock somewhere in the room. Invite the volunteers back inside and see how long it takes them to locate the hidden clock. Naturally, the class must be absolutely still so the searchers can hear the ticking.

If an alarm clock is not available, you might try the activity with a softly-playing portable radio or with a cooking timer.

TRY TO REMEMBER

The opening days of school are such a whirlwind of activity that some of your students may find it hard to concentrate. So here's a special game to help them do just that.

Show your class a large intricate picture, either from a big book, a poster, or a projection that you shine on the wall. Allow the class to study the picture for one full minute. Then remove the picture and see how many details each student can recall.

Ask them questions such as:

- How many people were in the picture?
- What color was the woman's dress?
- What was the boy carrying in his right hand?
- What animals were in the picture?
- How many people wore hats?

Children love this type of activity, so even if you forget to do it often, your class will remember to ask for it!

STUDENT TIME CAPSULE

Student Time Capsules are a super way to open and close the school year.

What goes in a time capsule? Almost anything! For starters, kids might enclose their information sheets from "Before and After" (p. 97) or "Taking the Class Census" (p. 15). They might also bury a photograph of their best friend, a wrapper from their favorite candy bar, or even a sock!

After every child has selected their objects, seal them tightly in tennis cans or similar containers. Find a spot outside where it's OK to bury them and make sure you remember where it is.

Then, at the end of the school year, unearth the containers and have the children inspect them. Your amateur archaeologists will be fascinated to discover the ways in which they've changed over the course of a year!

BULLETIN BOARD IDEAS

GROWING BULLETIN BOARDS

What do these bulletin boards have in common with all children? Give up? They both grow!

A Growing Bulletin Board is one that changes a little each day throughout the course of its one-week life span. Growing Bulletin Boards are a great way for new students to work together. So why not cultivate a few of your own during the opening weeks of school?

Here are some suggestions:

A Summer Vacation Board   Have children display objects that reflect their summer experiences and adventures.

Monday—Every student brings in an item representing a summer activity that they enjoyed. It might be a paper plate from a picnic, a seashell from a beach visit, a sneaker from summer camp, or a postcard from an out-of-town trip. The objects are attached to a bulletin board backdrop that has a space allotted for each student. Entitle the board "Our Summer Fun."

Tuesday—Students write brief captions that explain what their objects represent. The captions are placed under each object on the board.

Wednesday—Children think of something they'd like to do next summer, and display a second representative object next to the first.

Thursday—Children write captions for their second object, explaining what they'd like to do next summer.

Friday—Each student stands next to her display, reads her captions, and tells about her objects. Allow for a brief question-and-answer period after each presentation.

GETTING-TO-KNOW-YOU BOARD

  In this get-acquainted activity, you leave notes for your students to respond to with their own notes.

   Monday—Attach one envelope with each student's name on it to the bulletin board. Inside, leave a short note about yourself. For example, you might write: Dear _____ , I like to make my own kites and fly them. What things do you like to do? Your teacher, _____ .

   Tuesday—Have children write notes in response and leave them in their envelopes.

   Wednesday—Write a second note to each student, telling about an upcoming class activity. For example, you might write: Dear _____ , This week we will be making leaf rubbings as a science project. What else would you like to do in class this year? Your teacher, _____ .

   Thursday—Have children respond to the notes and leave them in their envelopes.

   Friday—Read some of the letters you received aloud to the class. Discuss your students hobbies or the activities they would like to do as a class.

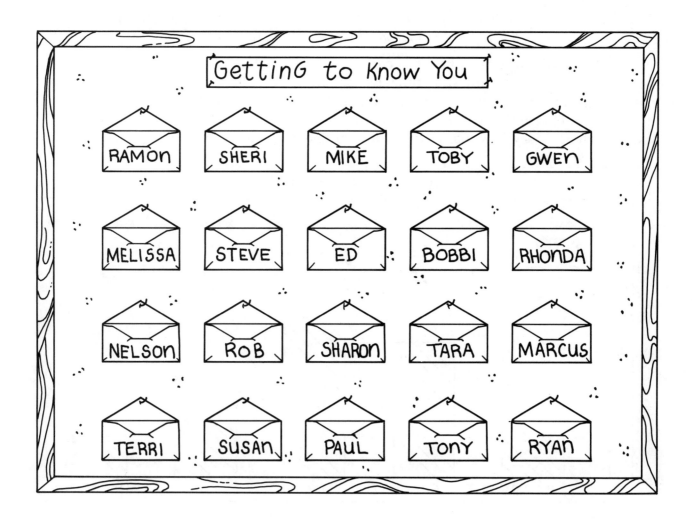

BAR GRAPH BOARD

Have children create a bar graph to indicate the results of a week-long survey.

Monday—Make five evenly-spaced horizontal marks going down the left-hand side of the bulletin board. Starting with the bottom mark, label them 5, 10, 15, 20, and 25. Then take a poll to determine how many kids in the class have pets. Using construction paper, cut a strip to represent that number. For example, if 14 kids have pets, make the strip almost long enough to reach the 15 mark on the bulletin board. Then staple the vertical strip to the left side of the board, and label it "Pets."

Tuesday—Have students tally the number of class members who have pet cats, and attach a second strip labeled "Cats" to indicate that number.

Wednesday—Have students tally the number of class members who have pet dogs, and attach a third strip labeled "Dogs" to indicate that number.

Thursday—Have students tally the number of class members who have pet fish, and attach a fourth strip labeled "Fish" to indicate that number.

Friday—Have students tally up the number of class members who have pet hamsters, and attach a strip labeled "Hamsters" to indicate that number.

Discuss with the class what they can learn from the bar graph. For example, twice as many students have cats than fish. Other possible questions to survey and graph during the week include: How many students ride the school bus each day, how many students buy their lunch each day, how many students wear sneakers each day?

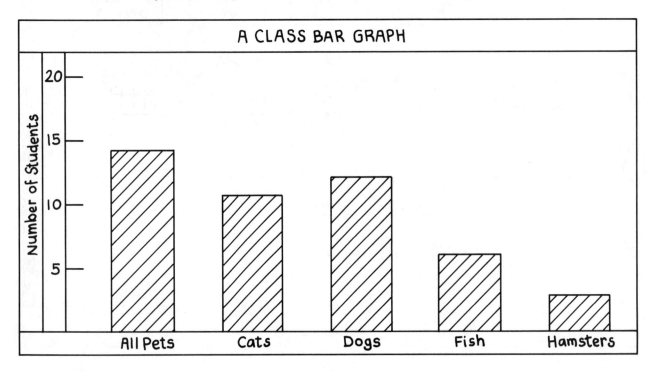

SCHOOL-MAP BOARD

Have your children visit a different part of the school each day and then draw a map of it to display.

Monday—Draw an outline of your classroom on a sheet of white paper, and place it on the bulletin board. Tell your children to study all of the things in your real classroom—windows, desks, etc.—and then draw them inside the outline.

Tuesday—Draw an outline of the cafeteria, and attach it to the bulletin board in proper relation to your classroom. Have your children fill in the outline with things such as tables, food counters, and vending machines.

Wednesday—Have students fill in an outline of the school library.

Thursday—Have students fill in an outline of the principal's office, nurse's office, auditorium, and/or other key locations in the building.

Friday—Have students complete their school map by filling in an outline of the school playground. Now, finding their way will be a lot easier.

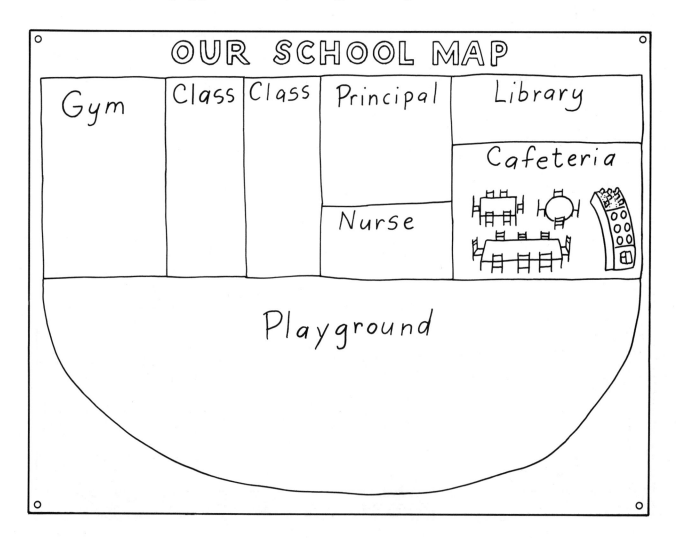

WELCOME-BACK-TO-SCHOOL SURPRISES

Surprise your children with a potpourri of special gifts—one for each day of the week.

Monday—Place an envelope on the bulletin board for each student. Write the student's name on it. Insert a bookmark with the student's name on it, leaving room for the child to draw his own picture on it.

Tuesday—Write a short note for each student that tells something you like about him. For example: "I liked the red shoes you were wearing yesterday." Leave the note in the envelope.

Wednesday—Insert a pencil with the student's name taped to the side.

Thursday—Insert a thank-you note for each student. For example: "Dear Sheri, Thank you for erasing the board yesterday."

Friday—Insert a special award for each student such as a Helpful Hero Award, or a Good Behavior Award.